THE ART OF
ISRAELI COOKING

THE ART OF ISRAELI COOKING

ORIGINAL ISRAELI RECIPES
NEVER BEFORE PUBLISHED AS WELL AS FAVORITE
TRADITIONAL DISHES - ALL KOSHER
Selected & edited by Chef Aldo Nahoum

JOHN GIFFORD LTD.

LONDON

JOHN GIFFORD LTD.
125 Charing Cross Road
London W.C.2.

Photography by : Ha nan Laskin

SBN : 7071212—X

Printed in Tel-Aviv, Israel

C O N T E N T S

5

19 **Diesut Couscous**
Cream of Wheat porridge with chicken
20 **Salat HaSharon**
Celery salad with eggs and spices
21 **Pashtidat Chatsilim**
Eggplant soufflé
22 **Chatzilim b'Rotav Agvaniot**
Eggplant in tomato sauce
23 **Tapochei Adama Memula'im**
Potatoes stuffed with meat
24 **Aley Kruv Memula'im**
Stuffed cabbage leaves in citrus sauce
25 **Salat Chatsilim**
Eggplant salad with lemon dressing
26 **Ta'arovet Beit Shean**
Artichokes and beans cocktail, in techina
sauce
27 **Shakshukah**
Egg and tomato mixture
28 **Latkes**
Sweetened potato pancakes
29 **Piramida Orez im Shakshukah**
Rice with egg and tomato mixture
30 **Kruvit HaMeshek**
Sweet-sour fried cauliflower
31 **Salat Mevushal**
Taverna Salad
32 **Kufta'ot Tapuchei Adamah**
Potato buttons
33 **Salat HaMizrach**
Vegetable salad, oriental style
34 **Rotev Agvaniyot Turkv**
Spiced ketchup
35 **Pashtidat Yerakot**
Potato pie with mushrooms and spinach
36 **Kaved Katsoots**
Chopped liver
37 **Kneidelach Tapuchei Adamah**
Potato balls
38 **Salat Hevron**
Eggplant with sweet red peppers
39 **Salat Tapuchei Adamah**
Potato salad in mayonnaise
40 **Orez Bombay**
Curried rice with nuts

6

7

62 **Dug Gruzia**
Russian carp
63 **Kudoorei Gefilte Fish**
Stuffed fish balls
64 **Dug b'Mitz Hadarim**
Fish in orange juice
65 **Gefilte Fish**
Stuffed carp, with almond flavor
66 **Ma'afeh Dugim**
Baked fish in tomato sauce
67 **Dug Yaffo**
Fish in white sauce
68 **Bakala Sfaradi**
Spiced hake
69 **Fillet Dug Sandal**
Sole in techina sauce
70 **Dug b'Rotev Charif**
Spiced fish in tomato sauce
71 **Dugim b'Limon**
Fish stew in lemon sauce

POULTRY pages 79 — 94

72 **Off HaAviv**
Chicken with peel of eggplants, peppers
and tomatoes
73 **Off Memulah b'Rotev Tapoozim**
Stuffed chicken in orange sauce
74 **Off B'Yayin V'Zaytim — Nusach Morocco**
Chicken cooked in wine and black olives
75 **Yonut HaShalom**
Stewed pigeons in wine
76 **Tzavar Hodu Mishpachti**
Stuffed turkey neck with nuts
77 **Shok Off Memulah**
Stuffed chicken legs, in chopped liver
78 **Kaved Off b'Nusach Yehudi**
Chicken liver in wine sauce and
mushrooms
79 **Off b'Afarsek**
Chicken breast with peaches
80 **Ketsitsot Off**
Ground chicken balls
81 **Chazeh Hodu Memulah**
Breast of turkey slices, stuffed with
mushrooms ↝

MEATS   pages 95 — 117

SWEETS & DESSERTS pages 118 — 132

INTRODUCTION

Israeli cooking as it is known today actually had its origins in 1948 when the state of Israel came into existence. As Israel's new citizens gathered together from all parts of the world, many brought with them the traditional recipes of their former Jewish communities.

There have been several influences on Jewish cooking over the centuries. Religion was one, as seen in the many special dishes prepared for particular holidays during the year. Another was the impact of the cooking habits within the countries where Jewish families settled. A good example of this is **gefilte fish** which originally was an Eastern European dish adopted and developed by Jewish cooks into the many forms in which it is now served — sweet, sour, garnished with nuts, or as fish-balls. Hungarian goulash has its Jewish version, and noodles — so often associated with Italian cooking — have a wide variety of kosher styles. Still another influence on Jewish food was the cooking traditions of original Jewish dishes kept by house-wives who over the years carefully preserved the treasured recipes. In Israel one can find them all. Israeli cooking encompasses all these influences and anyone who appreciates good eating can find a lot of enjoyment sampling the various dishes.

The Art of Israeli Cooking features two types of recipes — traditional dishes which have now become favorites, and new, original recipes never before published, which have come into being in Israel over the last twenty years.

Grateful appreciation goes to the enthusiastic team of researchers who traveled around Israel collecting the traditional recipes from the various communities. Many of them had never been recorded before, since they were passed verbally from mother to daughter, and in a fast-growing state like Israel, were in danger of being lost altogether.

The new recipes were created by the finest team of chefs Israel could offer. Chef Aldo Nahoum, the editor of this book, began his career in Tripoli twenty-five years ago. He emigrated to Israel, and currently runs two highly successful restaurants in Tel Aviv. He is a life member of the seven-hundred-year-old **Chain des Rotisseurs.**

Chef Roger was born in North Africa, emigrated to France where he began his cooking career, and from there moved on to Israel. He now manages his own restaurant in Jaffa. For many years he was the gastronomical advisor to the **Chain des Rotisseurs,** and is considered Israel's top authority on gourmet food.
Chef Mordechai emigrated from Rumania to Israel and has achieved outstanding success by winning numerous awards for his original recipes.

All the dishes in **The Art of Israeli Cooking** can be easily prepared in the average kitchen. The cooking time indicated on each recipe is recommended by the chefs, but the preparation time was averaged out for the housewife working under normal conditions.

KERMAN/KERMAN

Vegetables & Salads

SALAT HADAR

ORANGE & GREENS — COCKTAIL SALAD

NEW

Preparing time: 20 minutes. Serves 6

---

1 head of fennel • 1 orange • 7 fresh lettuce leaves • 2 carrots, peeled • ½ cup salad oil • Juice of 1 lemon • Salt • Pepper

---

Cut lettuce leaves finely. Peel the fennel. Divide into two, and cut into thin slices. Slice carrots thinly. Place prepared ingredients in salad bowl, and sprinkle with salt and pepper. Add oil and lemon juice, and decorate with orange slices.

2   AVOCADO PRI ARTZENU

AVOCADO COCKTAIL IN LIQUEUR SAUCE

NEW

Preparing time: 15 minutes. Serves 6

---

3 medium-size avocadoes • 2 apples, peeled and cubed •
2 pears, peeled and cubed • 2 bananas, peeled and cubed
• 2 oranges, peeled and cubed • 6 cherries • 1 jigger
of any desired liqueur

Divide each avocado in half, and remove pits. Combine all
fruit, except the cherries, and liqueur, and mix well. Stuff each
avocado half with the fruit cocktail. Decorate with a cherry.
Serve as an entrée.

3   ALLEH GEFEN MEMULA'IM

DOLMADES

Grape leaves, stuffed with rice

TRADITIONAL among Greek Jews

Preparing time: 20 minutes. Cooking time: 60-90 mins. **Serves 5**

---

24 large grape leaves • 2 heaping cups (20 tbs.) uncooked
rice • 1½ cups oil • Juice of 2 lemons • 2 tbs. parsley,
chopped • 1 tsp. anise • 3 ozs. fresh mint, chopped • 1
large onion • Salt • Pepper

Wash the grape leaves, and place in a bowl. Pour boiling water over, and let stand covered for 10 mins. before draining. Place rice in a strainer, and wash under running water. Fry onion in ½ cup oil, until golden. Add the rice and spices, and fry for 10 mins. Remove from heat, add all the other ingredients except lemon juice, and remainder of oil, and mix. On inside of each of 20 grape leaves place 1 tbs. of the mixture, fold each leaf tightly (like a small parcel), and squeeze in the palm of hand. This will remove excess liquids, and also ensure the grape leaves will stay rolled up during cooking, and they need not be tied. Pour the remainder of the oil in a shallow saucepan. Spread remaining four grape leaves flat at the bottom of pan, and on them tightly pack the stuffed grape leaves. Pour over lemon juice and water to cover. Place small plate over leaves, to prevent them moving during cooking. Cover saucepan with lid, and bring to boil. Reduce heat, and let simmer for 1-1½ hours. Serve cold, as first course or side dish to a main course, with white wine or rosé.
See photograph on page 46.

4   CHARSHOFAY NATSERET

DELICATESS NAZARETH

Artichokes with meat mixture

NEW

Preparing time: 35 minutes. Cooking time: 50 minutes. Serves 6

---

4 artichokes • 2 cloves garlic • 2 ozs. pine nuts • 1 lb. fillet of beef, sliced • Oil for frying • Grill spice • Black pepper • Salt

---

Place meat in a pan with oil and 2 cloves garlic. Fry on very low heat, while gradually adding a cup of lukewarm water. Cook for ½ hour. Remove artichoke leaves and chokes. Take care to leave part of the stalk. Wash the hearts well, and divide

each into quarters. Add artichoke pieces to meat, another cup
of lukewarm water, and pine nuts. Sprinkle with salt, grill spice
and black pepper, cover, and let simmer for 20 mins., stirring
from time to time during cooking.
Serve as main dish, with dry red wine.

5   KISHU'IM B'TA'AM CHAMUTZ

SOUR SALAD

Sour Summer Squash Salad

NEW

Preparing time: 10 minutes. Cooking time: 15 minutes. Serves 6

10 ozs. young summer squashes • 1 hard-boiled egg •
1 medium cucumber pickle • ½ tsp. mustard • 2 tbs.
vinegar • 3 tbs. mayonnaise • 1½ cups water • Salt •
Pepper • Red paprika

Wash squashes, and divide each into four long sections. Boil
these in water and vinegar for 15 mins. Cool and drain. In a
bowl mix mayonnaise, mustard, grated egg, cucumber, salt and
pepper. Place squash slices in bowl, and mix.
Garnish with red paprika, and serve as an appetizer.

6   MATZIAS

SUMMER SQUASH, STUFFED WITH CHEESE

TRADITIONAL for Spanish Jews

Preparing time: 30 minutes. Cooking time: 15 mins. Serves 5-6

2 lbs. young summer squashes • ½ lb. Cheddar or Parmesan cheese, grated • 3 eggs • 6 tbs. tomato purée • 2 cloves garlic, minced • ½ cup water • Oil for frying

Wash squashes, and cut each one into half, along its length. Scoop out inside, leaving shell about ½ inch thick. Mix well cheese and beaten egg. Stuff half squashes with cheese mixture, and fry in oil (stuffed side downwards) until golden. Turn, and fry second side until golden. Remove, and place in a shallow saucepan. Add tomato purée, garlic and water, and let simmer over low heat for 15 minutes.
Serve hot as first course, or main course with baked potatoes.

7   MEDROTA

EGGPLANT IN CHEESE

TRADITIONAL for Spanish Jews

Preparing time: 15-20 minutes. Cooking time: 15 mins. Serves 4

1 medium-size eggplant • 1¾ cups of Cheddar or Parmesan cheese • 4 cloves garlic, whole • Oil for frying • Salt • ½ cup water

Peel the eggplant, and cube. Cut cheese into cubes, and fry together with garlic in a little oil, until light brown. Add eggplant cubes to pan, sprinkle with salt, and mix well. Add water, and let simmer over low heat for 15 minutes.
Serve as first course, with white wine or rosé.

8   GIVOLEH CHARSHOF

ARTICHOKE FINGERS

Artichoke stalks, in lemon juice

NEW

Preparing time: 10 mins. Cooking time: 45-55 mins. Serves 5-6

8-10 young artichoke stalks • 4 cloves garlic, fried • Juice of ½ lemon • 3 tbs. oil for frying • Red hot pepper • Salt • 2 cups lukewarm water

---

Remove outer peel and fibres of stalks. Wash, and place stalks in shallow saucepan. Add oil, red pepper, salt to taste, and garlic. Pour in water, and let simmer over low heat for 45 mins., until stalks are tender. Shortly before stalks are ready, add lemon juice. Continue to cook until most of the liquid has evaporated, and sauce has formed at the bottom of the saucepan. Serve as appetizer, or side dish with meat.

9   CHATZIL AFOU'I

EGGPLANT SOUFFLÉ

Baked eggplants with cheese mixture

TRADITIONAL for Bulgarian Jews

Preparing time: 15 minutes. Baking time: 20 mins. Serves 6-8

---

2 large eggplants • 1 ⅓ cups cream cheese • 1¼ cups of Cheddar or Parmesan cheese, grated • 2 eggs • Salt • ⅓ cup margarine

---

Wash eggplants, and grill them over flame, or in grill. Remove peel by hand. Place eggplants in a glass bowl, and mash. Add cream cheese, half of the grated cheese, eggs and salt to taste. Mix well.

Grease a baking dish with a little margarine. Pour in eggplant mixture, sprinkle with remainder of grated cheese, and dot with remainder of margarine. Bake in a hot oven for 20 minutes, or until cheese melts.

Serve as first course.

10   PRASAH

LEEK BALLS

TRADITIONAL for Bulgarian Jews

Preparing time: 30 minutes. Cooking time: 30 minutes. Serves 6

> 2 large leeks • 5 ozs. lean beef • 2 eggs • ½ slice white bread, soaked in water and drained • 1 egg, hard-boiled • Oil for frying • Breadcrumbs • Salt • Pepper

Cook leeks in water for 15 minutes, drain and let cool. In a bowl mince together meat, cooked leeks, hard-boiled egg and bread. Mix well, and add two beaten eggs, seasoning and breadcrumbs. Form into balls, and fry in oil.

Serve as first course, or a side dish to the main course.
See photograph on page 45.

11   AGVANYIOT MEMULA'OT

STUFFED TOMATOES WITH CHEESE

NEW

Preparing time: 15 minutes. Serves 5

---

5 firm tomatoes • ½ cup cottage cheese • 2 tbs. mayonnaise • 2 eggs, hard-boiled • 3 spring onions, chopped • 1 cucumber pickle, finely chopped • 2 tbs sour milk • 5 lettuce leaves • Salt • Pepper • 5 black olives

---

Wash all the vegetables. Slice off tops of tomatoes, and set aside tops. Scoop out flesh of tomatoes. Mix the flesh with hard-boiled egg, spring onion and pickle. Add cheese, most of the sour milk, mayonnaise, salt and pepper, and blend into an even mixture. Stuff tomatoes with cheese mixture. Replace tops on stuffed tomatoes, and arrange each on one lettuce leaf. Pour remainder of cheese mixture, diluted with remainding sour milk, over and around, and decorate with black olive.
Serve as first course, or for light meals.

12 MATBEYLAH

EGGPLANT DIPS

Eggplant in techina sauce

TRADITIONAL for Oriental Jews

Preparing time: 15 minutes. Cooking time: 5 mins. Serves 4-5

---

1 medium-size eggplant • ½ cup ready-made techina • Juice of ½ lemon • Parsley, chopped • ½ clove garlic, minced • Salt

---

Grill the eggplant over a flame for about 10 mins., until tender. Remove the peel by hand, mash the eggplant, and add techina. Mix well, and add garlic, salt to taste, lemon juice and parsley. Mix to smooth consistency.
Serve as main course, or salad.

13   ZAYTIM MEVUSHALIM

COOKED OLIVES

TRADITIONAL for Oriental Jews

Preparing time: 10-15 mins. Cooking time: 30 mins. Serves 5

> 1 lb. green olives pitted • 6 cloves garlic • Red pepper •
> 3 tbs. oil for frying • Juice of ½ lemon • Parsley, chopped
> • Salt • 1 cup water • 1 lemon slice.

Sauté garlic in oil, until golden. Add red pepper, water, parsley
and olives, and cook over very low heat for 30 minutes, until
most of the liquid evaporates. Add lemon juice shortly before
dish is ready.
Decorate with a lemon slice, and serve as appetizer, or with
grilled or stuffed chicken.

14   PILPEL HAKFAR HAYAROK

GREEN VILLAGE SNOWFALL

Stuffed peppers with rice, in sour cream dressing.

NEW

Preparing time: 20 minutes. Cooking time: 60 minutes. Serves 5

> 10 green peppers • 5 ozs. rice, uncooked • 8 ozs. minced
> meat • 1 large ripe tomato, peeled and grated • 3 ozs.
> tomato purée • 1 large onion, chopped • 2 tbs. parsley,
> chopped • ½ cup oil for frying • 1 tbs. mint, chopped •
> 2 cups water • 1 tsp. sugar • Salt • Pepper • 1 cup
> parvé sour cream

Slice the tops off the peppers, and put aside. Extract core and
seeds, then wash and put aside.

Sauté onion in oil, add uncooked rice, and continue to fry for a while. Add parsley, mint, grated tomato, salt, pepper and meat. Mix well. Stuff peppers ¾ full with mixture.

Replace tops on peppers, and carefully pack them in a shallow saucepan. Pour water over, bring to a boil, reduce heat and continue to cook for ½ hour. Add tomato purée and sugar, and cook for another 30 minutes.

Serve 1-2 peppers per portion. Pour parvé cream over each pepper.

15 CHARSHOFIM MEMULA'IM NUSACH YEHUDAI SURIA

STUFFED ARTICHOKES

TRADITIONAL for Syrian Jews

Preparing time: 30 minutes. Cooking time: 45 minutes. Serves 6

---

12 artichokes • 1 tin anchovies • 1 onion, finely chopped • 1½ cups rice • 3 tbs. oil for frying • Salt • Juice of ½ lemon • 2 tbs. bread crumbs • White pepper

---

Cut off artichoke stems, remove leaves and the choke, leaving the hollowed-out heart. Place in salted water, add lemon juice, and cook until soft, about 15 mins. Be careful not to overcook. Remove hearts from saucepan, cool, and dry on paper towel. Sauté onions on medium heat, until golden. Add anchovies, cut into pieces. While frying, mash mixture in saucepan with wooden spoon and stir until texture is even. Add rice, a pinch of pepper, salt to taste, about ½ cup water, and continue to cook for about 20 mins., until rice is ready. Place rice in another dish, and set aside to cool. Stuff artichoke hearts with balls of rice.

Pour ½ cup water and 2 tbs. oil in a baking dish, carefully place stuffed artichokes in dish, sprinkle with breadcrumbs and a few drops of oil on each artichoke. Bake in hot oven for 10 mins. Serve hot as first or main course, with red wine.

See photograph on page 35.

16   TA'AROVET OREZ GONDOLA

GONDOLA COCKTAIL

Rice cocktail, with smoked goose & vegs.
(note: turkey can be substituted)

NEW

Preparing time: 30 minutes. Cooking time: 45 minutes. Serves 6

---

1 smoked goose (or turkey), whole • 1 heaping cup of rice • 10 ozs. shelled peas • 1 spring onion • Parsley, chopped • 1½ cups chicken broth • Oil for frying • 1-2 tbs. margarine • Salt • Pepper

---

Grease a saucepan with margarine, and fry goose, with onion and parsley, until golden in color.
Add water to second saucepan and cook peas on high heat until tender (but not mushy). Remove, and add to goose.
Fry rice in oil separately until golden, and add to goose.
Add stock gradually to saucepan, salt and pepper to taste, reduce heat, and cook on medium heat until rice is done.
Serve as main dish, with fresh vegetable salad and white wine.

17   TA'AROVET YEREK UBAITSIM B'NUSACH YEHUDEI HAMIZRACH

TRADITIONAL ORIENTAL

Eastern salad

TRADITIONAL

Preparing time: 10 minutes. Cooking time: 25 minutes. Serves 6

---

2 lbs. tomatoes, sliced • 3 large green peppers • 2 chili peppers • 5 cloves garlic, minced • 12 eggs • Oil • Salt

---

Remove seeds of peppers, rinse, and cut into long strips. In frying pan, heat oil. Place tomatoes, peppers, garlic and some salt in hot oil, and cover pan. Leave on low heat, stir occasionally until vegetables are cooked.

Spread vegetables evenly into a baking dish. Place raw eggs on vegetables. Sprinkle with salt, and bake in moderate oven for 10 mins., until eggs are hard.

Serve two eggs per portion, as first or main course.

18   SALAT HASTAV

FALL SEASON SALAD

Bean and tuna fish salad in wine sauce

NEW

Preparing time: 15 minutes. Cooking time: 15 mins. Serves 5-6

---

2 lbs. green beans • 4 ozs. tin Tuna fish, flaked • ¾ cup wine-vinegar • Pinch of basil • 1 tbs. parsley, chopped • 2 cloves garlic, minced • 6 anchovy fillets • Olive oil • 1 medium onion, chopped • Salt • Pepper

---

In a deep bowl pour wine-vinegar, chopped parsley and basil. Put finely-chopped onion into a wet cloth, and squeeze into the bowl. Add the garlic, and flaked Tuna fish.

Cook the beans in salted water, and add to salad while still hot. Add anchovies, cover bowl, and set cool.

Before serving, mix in oil, salt and pepper to taste.

19 DIESUT COUSCOUS

CHICKEN PORRIDGE

Cream of Wheat porridge, with chicken

TRADITIONAL for Tunisian Jews

Preparing time: 20 minutes. Cooking time: 35 minutes. Serves 6

> 3 heaping cups Cream of Wheat, sifted • ½ cup margarine
> • 1 onion, chopped and fried • Grilled chicken (skinned)
> chopped • Salt

Pour gradually 1 cup water on Cream of Wheat, and mix in well.
Pour this mixture into the top of a double-boiler and place
on boilers' pan half-filled with water. Take care that the water
in the saucepan does not touch the Cream of Wheat. Let the
water boil on medium heat for 15 minutes. Remove from heat,
and let cool.
Add gradually 2 cups water to Cream of Wheat, stirring constantly. Thoroughly mix in the margarine, place top and contents
over saucepan of water, and steam for another 20 minutes. Mix
chopped chicken, fried onion and salt in the Cream of Wheat.
Serve hot, as main dish, with Pernod.

20 SALAT HASHARON

SHARON VALLEY SALAD

Celery salad, with eggs and spices

NEW

Preparing time: 10 minutes. Cooking time: 10 minutes. Serves 6

> 2 eggs, hard-boiled • 4 small celery stalks • 5-6 black
> olives • ½ cup olive oil • 2 tbs. vinegar • 1½ tsp. mustard
> • Salt • Pepper

Peel and wash celery stalks, and cut into thin slices. Place slices in a bowl, pour oil over, and let marinate for 1 hour. Slice eggs, pit the olives and slice into rings. Add these ingredients to salad in bowl. Sprinkle over salt and pepper to taste. Blend mustard and vinegar, add to the salad, and mix well. Transfer to salad bowl, and serve.

21   PASHTIDAT CHATSILIM

EGGPLANT SOUFFLÉ

TRADITIONAL for Persian Jews

Preparing time: 25 minutes. Cooking time: 40 minutes. Serves 6

> 2 large eggplants • ½ cup oil for frying • 3 eggs • 1 tbs. margarine • ½ tsp. garlic powder • Juice of 1 lemon • Salt • Pepper • Flour or breadcrumbs

Wash and cut unpeeled eggplants in ½ inch thick slices, sprinkle with salt and let stand for quarter of an hour. Drain off excess liquid, and fry in hot oil until golden. Let cool. Separate eggs. Place eggplant slices in bowl, mash, adding garlic powder, salt and pepper, egg yolks and lemon juice. Beat the egg whites until stiff, fold into mixture, and mix well. Grease a baking or soufflé dish with margarine, sprinkle with flour or breadcrumbs. Pour in the mixture, and bake in hot oven for 5 minutes. Reduce heat and continue to bake until a crust is formed on top of soufflé. Grated cheese (Parmesan) can be added before baking, if desired.
Cut into slices and serve hot, as first course.

22 CHATZILIM B'ROTEV AGVANIOT

EGGPLANT IN TOMATO SAUCE

NEW

Preparing time: 15 minutes. Cooking time: 10 minutes. Serves 4

---

1 medium eggplant, peeled and sliced • 3 cloves garlic, minced • 3 ozs. tomato purée • Salt • Pepper • Oil for frying

---

Fry eggplant in hot oil. Remove and place in small saucepan. Sprinkle minced garlic on eggplant slices, add salt and pepper to taste, and tomato purée. Simmer over low heat for 10 mins. Serve hot or cold, as first course.

23 TAPOCHEI ADAMA MEMULA'IM

POTATOES STUFFED WITH MEAT

TRADITIONAL for Bukhara Jews

Preparing time: 45 minutes. Cooking time: 45 minutes. Serves 5

---

1 lb. beef, minced • 1 slice white bread, soaked in water, and drained • 2 eggs • 1 tbs. parsley, chopped • 1 small onion, chopped • 5 large potatoes peeled • 6 cloves garlic • ½ tsp. black pepper • ¼ tsp. saffron • Oil for frying • Flour • Water • Salt

---

Mix well meat, bread, onion, parsley, 1 egg, salt and pepper. Set aside. Cut potatoes in two, lengthwise. Scoop out the middle part of each half, and set aside. Stuff the hollowed potatoes with meat mixture, coat in flour, then in a beaten egg, and fry in oil until golden. After frying is completed, pour remainder of frying oil into a saucepan. In it sauté garlic, add scooped-out portions of potatoes.

On top arrange the fried stuffed potatoes, season with salt, pepper and saffron, and put in water to cover. Cook over high heat, until boiling point is reached, reduce heat and continue to cook over low heat until potatoes are done.

Serve as main course, with pickles.

24   ALEY KRUV MEMULA'IM

STUFFED CABBAGE LEAVES IN CITRUS SAUCE

NEW

Preparing time: 15 mins. Cooking time: 75 mins. Serves: 10-12

> 1 cabbage (approx. 1 lb.) • ½ lb. minced beef • ½ cup rice • Parsley, chopped • 6 cloves garlic, sliced • Juice of ½ lemon • Juice of ½ orange • ½ tsp. sugar • Mint, chopped • 2 tbs. oil for frying • Salt • Black pepper

Separate cabbage leaves, and arrange in a deep saucepan. Pour over water to cover, and bring to a boil. Remove from heat. Mix rice and mince meat, add parsley, salt, pepper and sugar. Continue to mix until texture obtained.

On each cabbage leaf arrange 1 tbs. of meat mixture. Roll leaf, and squeeze in palm of hand to extract liquid. Arrange stuffed leaves in a shallow pan, add garlic, mint, salt, pepper and oil. Pour over water to cover, and let simmer over low heat for 60 mins. Before serving, add juice of lemon and orange, and cook for another 5-10 mins. 2 tablespoons tomato ketehup may be spread on if desired

Serve as first course, or as main course, with white wine. See photograph on page 47.

25   SALAT CHATSILIM

EGGPLANT SALAD

Eggplant salad with lemon dressing

TRADITIONAL for Greek Jews

Preparing time: 20 minutes. Cooking time: 10 minutes. Serves 8

> 1 large eggplant • 1 large onion, chopped • Juice of 1
> lemon • 2 tbs. parsley, chopped • 3 tbs. tomato purée •
> 1 cup olive oil • Salt • Pepper

Wash eggplant and grill over an open flame. When soft, peel
by hand and wash in glass bowl, draining off excessive liquid.
Add chopped onion, lemon juice, parsley, tomato purée, salt
and pepper. Mix well, preferably with electric blender. Add
oil — drop by drop blending all the while.
Serve as first course on fresh lettuce leaves. Decorate with
black olives and tomato slices.

26   TA'AROVET BEIT SHEAN

BEIT SHEAN COCKTAIL

Artichokes and beans cocktail, in techina sauce

NEW

Preparing time: 15 minutes. Cooking time: 2 hours, Serves 6

> 6 artichokes • 1 cup dried navy beans or chickpeas •
> Juice of 1 lemon • 1 tin ready-made techina • 2 cloves
> garlic, minced • Salt • Pepper

Soak dried beans in water for 12 hours.
Place beans in saucepan with water, add salt and pepper.

Bring to boil, and continue for about 30 minutes.
Dispose of artichoke leaves and chokes, and then cube the hearts. Add artichoke hearts to saucepan, and continue to cook together over a low flame until beans are tender. Remove from saucepan, drain and let cool.
Combine techina sauce, lemon juice, salt, pepper, and garlic. Mix well. Pour the sauce over artichokes and beans cocktail. Serve as first course.

27   SHAKSHUKAH

EGG AND TOMATO MIXTURE

TRADITIONAL for Yemenite Jews

Preparing time: 10 minutes. Cooking time: 25 minutes. Serves 6

---

6 eggs • 5 ripe tomatoes • 2 cloves garlic • ½ green pepper • Oil for frying • 2 ozs. tomato purée or ketchup • Salt • Pepper

---

Cut tomatoes into squares and the peppers into thin strips. Heat some oil in a deep saucepan. Fry vegetables and garlic, until tomatoes are tender. Reduce heat. Mash tomatoes with fork. Add tomato purée or ketchup, salt and pepper to taste. After 10 mins. carefully break in eggs, cover with lid and continue to cook on low heat for another 15 minutes. If liquid evaporates during cooking, add a little warm water.
Serve one egg per person, with no side dishes.

28   LATKES

SWEETENED POTATO PANCAKES

TRADITIONAL

Preparing time: 30 minutes. Cooking time: 20 minutes. Serves 6

---

6 large potatoes, peeled and grated • 1 onion, grated •
1 large apple, grated • 3 eggs • ½ tsp. cinnamon • 2 tbs.
flour • Oil for frying • Salt • Pepper

Mix potatoes, apple and onion. Beat eggs into mixture, add
flour and seasoning. Shape into pancakes.
Heat oil in pan, and drop in pancakes. Fry until brown and
crisp on both sides.
Serve with jam, or sprinkle with sugar.

29   PIRAMIDA OREZ IM SHAKSHUKA

RICE PYRAMIDS

Rice with egg and tomato mixture

TRADITIONAL for Moroccan Jews

Preparing time: 20 minutes. Cooking time: 30 minutes. Serves 6

---

2 cups rice • 4 cups water • 1 tsp. salt • 3 tbs. margarine

Wash the rice thoroughly, and strain. In a saucepan bring to
boil 4 cups of water, and salt. Place rice in water, and stir a
few times. When half the liquid is absorbed, reduce heat, and
cover. Simmer for 20 minutes.
Heat margarine in a frying pan, pour it over the rice, and
continue to simmer in covered pan for another 10 minutes.
Shakshukah — See recipe no. 27

Serve on a flat dish, forming rice into pyramid shapes. At the peak of each pyramid scoop out a hollow, and pour in 2 tbs. of shakshuka mixture. Decorate base of pyramid with sauce remaining in pan.
Serve as a main course.
See photograph on page 48.

30   KRUVIT HAMESHEK

COUNTRY CAULIFLOWER

Sweet-sour fried cauliflower

NEW

Preparing time: 15 minutes. Cooking time: 20 minutes. Serves 5

---

1 large cauliflower • 1 cup water • 1 egg • ¼ cup oil for frying • 4 tbs. flour • 3 tbs. lemon juice • 1 tsp. sugar • 1 clove garlic, minced • Salt

---

Divide cauliflower into flowerets. Put in saucepan, add salt and water to cover. Boil for 10 minutes. Drain.
Prepare a batter from flour, one-third cup water, egg and a pinch of salt. Coat cauliflower flowerets in the batter and fry in hot oil. Remove to a shallow saucepan, add ⅔ cup water, lemon juice, garlic and sugar. Simmer for 15 mins. on low heat.
Serve as first course, decorated with lemon slices.

31   SALAT MEVUSHAL

TAVERNA SALAD

Cooked salad

TRADITIONAL for Greek Jews

Preparing time: 25 minutes. Cooking time: 60 minutes. Serves 5

---

1 large kohlrabi • 1 large summer squash • 2 large
tomatoes • 2 sweet peppers, 1 green and 1 red • 1 large
onion • 1 large potato • 1 tbs. parsley. chopped • ¼ cup
oil for frying • Salt • Pepper

Peel and wash vegetables. Cube.
Fry onion in oil until golden. Add the remainder of the cubed
vegetables, parsley and seasoning. Pour in water to cover
vegetables, and bring to boil. Cover. Continue to stew over
low heat for one hour, or until vegetables are soft.
Serve as side dish, with meat and potatoes, or as first course
with old port wine.

32   KUFTA'OT TAPUCHEI ADAMAH

POTATO BUTTONS

TRADITIONAL for Jews of India

Preparing time: 15 minutes. Cooking time: 40 minutes. Serves 6

---

2 lbs. potatoes • 2 tbs. flour • ½ lb. ground beef • 1
onion, chopped • 4 tsp. oil for frying • 2 eggs • Matzo meal
• Salt • Pepper • Cinnamon • Saffron

Wash the potatoes, and cook in their jackets, in salted water.

Remove when cooked, and let cool. Peel and mash. Add flour, matzo meal (according to need), eggs, and form into dough. Heat 4 tsp. oil in a frying pan, fry onion, add minced meat, salt and the spices. Add a little water, and simmer on low heat until meat is cooked. Let cool.

Form small balls (¾ inch) from the potato dough, make a small hole in each, and stuff with meat. Close the hole, and press the potato ball gently with both hands, forming a flat eliptical shape. Coat balls in matzo meal, and fry in hot oil.

Serve for supper with hot tea.

33   SALAT HAMIZRACH

ORIENTAL SALAD

Vegetable salad, oriental style

TRADITIONAL

Preparing time: 20 minutes. Serves 6

---

2 large tomatoes • 2 small cucumbers • 1 small chili pepper • 1 sweet green pepper • 1 medium onion stem • 2 cloves garlic, crushed • 1 tbs. parsley, chopped • 1 tbs. mint, chopped • Salt • Pepper • ¼ cup olive oil • Juice of 1 lemon

---

Wash all vegetables well, and cut into small cubes. Add all other ingredients, and mix well. Place in refrigerator half an hour before serving.

34 ROTEV AGVANIYOT TURKY

SPICED KETCHUP

TRADITIONAL for Turkish Jews

Preparing time: 10 minutes. Cooking time: 10 minutes. Serves 6

---

2 cups tomatoes, mashed • 2 level tbs. flour • 1 medium onion, minced • 1 green pepper, diced • 3 tbs. oil for frying • 1 tbs. parsley, chopped • 2 tbs. water • Pinch of chili powder • Salt

---

Sauté onion in oil, add flour, stirring steadily. Add tomatoes, green pepper, parsley, salt, chili powder and water. Stir well and cook over low heat for 10 minutes.
Serve with meats, fish, macaroni or boiled rice.
See photograph on page 36.

35 PASHTIDAT YERAKOT

MUSHROOM MOUSSAKA

Potato pie with mushrooms and spinach

NEW

Preparing time: 15 minutes. Cooking time: 30 minutes. Serves 6

---

4 eggs • 1¼ lb. potatoes, peeled • 2¼ cups mushrooms • ¼ lb. spinach • Salt • Juice of ½ lemon

---

Cook potatoes in saucepan with water, until tender. Remove, mash the potatoes, add 1 egg, and mix.
Rinse mushrooms thoroughly, place in a saucepan with water and lemon juice, and cook for 10 mins. Remove, let cool, and

chop finely, or mince. Add in 1 egg, and mix well.
Rinse spinach well, and cook in salty water. Remove from saucepan, drain, chop finely, add 1 egg, and mix.
Grease a baking dish, place in a layer of potato, about half-inch thick. Top with all the mushrooms, place over another layer of potato.
Top with all the spinach, and cover with remainder of potato.
Beat 1 egg well, pour over moussaka, and bake in a moderate oven for 10 minutes.
Serve as first course, or side dish to meat.

36   KAVED KATSOOTS

CHOPPED LIVER

TRADITIONAL for Polish Jews

Preparing time: 15 minutes. Cooking time: 20 minutes. Serves 8

---

10 chicken livers • 1 onion, grated • 2 hard-boiled eggs • 1 tsp. parsley, chopped • 2 tbs. chicken fat • Salt • Pepper • 1 lemon, sliced

---

Place chicken livers in pan, with water to cover. Add pinch of salt, and cook till tender. Remove to cool. Chop together with eggs, season and add grated onion. Mix with chicken fat. Serve on lettuce leaves, and garnish with parsley.
Serve as first course, with red wine. Decorate with lemon slices.

37   KNEIDELACH TAPUCHEI ADAMAH

POTATO KNEIDELS

Potato balls

TRADITIONAL for European Jews

Preparing time: 20 minutes. Cooking time: 35 minutes. Serves 6

> 3 cups raw potatoes, grated • 2 eggs • 2 tbs. matzo meal
> • 1 tbs. onion, grated • ¼ cup potato • Flour • 1 tsp. salt

Separate eggs. Beat yolks, and add salt and onion. Stir grated potato and matzo meal into potato flour, and add to egg yolks. Beat egg whites until stiff, and fold in. Form mixture into balls. Drop carefully into salted water. Remove balls when they rise to the top. (Cooking should not take more than 25 minutes). Place balls in oven for 10 minutes before serving.
Serve as side dish to main course, or as first course.

38   SALAT HEVRON

HEBRON HILLS SALAD

Eggplant with sweet red peppers

NEW

Preparing time: 10 minutes. Cooking time: 15 minutes. Serves 6

> 1 lb. eggplant • 1 sweet red pepper • 4 cloves garlic •
> 1 tbs. vinegar • Salt • Pepper

Grill eggplant over flame or grill, for 15 minutes. Cool and peel by hand. Mince eggplant together with red peppers and garlic. Mix well, add vinegar, seasoning, and mix again.
Serve as first course, or as a side dish to main course.

39   SALAT TAPUCHEI ADAMAH

POTATO SALAD

Potato salad in mayonnaise

TRADITIONAL for Hungarian Jews

Preparing time: 20 minutes. Serves 6

---

4 large potatoes, cooked • 2 carrots, cooked • 7 ozs. cauliflower, semi-cooked • 1 cup green peas, shelled and cooked • ½ cup mayonnaise • Juice of ½ lemon • 1 hard-boiled egg, chopped • 2 black olives, pitted and finely chopped • Parsley, chopped • Salt • Pepper

---

Cut potatoes, carrots and cauliflower into small cubes. Prepare a dressing of mayonnaise, lemon juice, salt and pepper. Add the chopped egg, olives, green peas and cubed vegetables. Mix well and put in refrigerator for about 1 - 2 hours. Before serving arrange in shallow dish and decorate with some chopped parsley. Serve as first course, or side dish with fried chicken.

40   OREZ BOMBAY

CURRIED RICE WITH NUTS

TRADITIONAL for Jews of India

Preparing time: 30 minutes. Cooking time: 30 minutes. **Serves 8**

---

2 cups rice • 1 tsp. saffron • 1 tsp. curry powder • 3 ozs. walnuts, chopped • ⅔ cup seedless raisins • ¼ cup oil for frying • 4 cups water • Salt

---

In a saucepan bring to boil water, salt, curry and saffron. Rinse

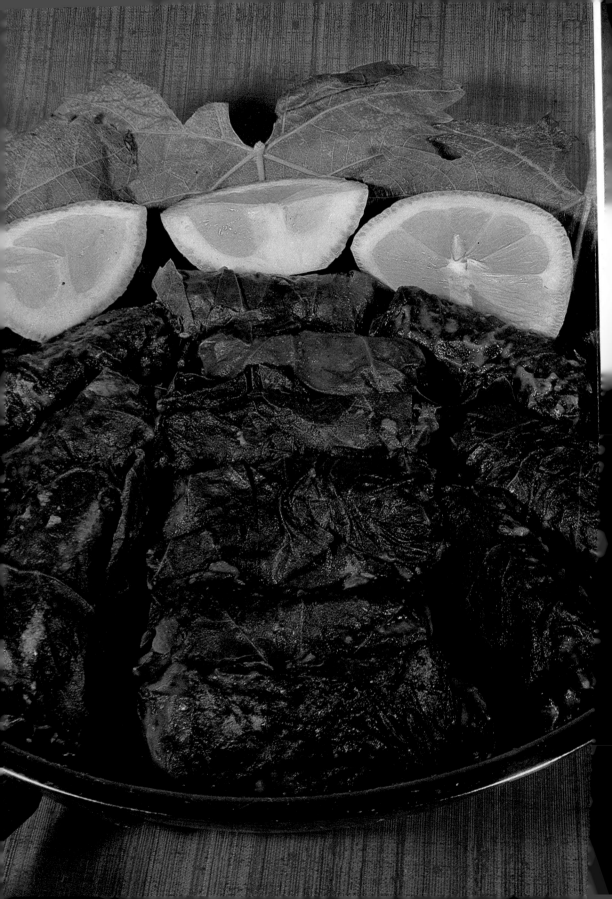

rice thoroughly, add to saucepan, and cook for 10 - 15 minutes. Take care to remove foam forming on top, so that rice will remain clear. Remove from heat and drain. Place in a bowl. Rinse raisins in water.

Heat oil in a pan, sauté nuts and remove. Place in raisins, and sauté until brownish. Remove and pour a little of the heated oil over rice. Garnish with fried nuts and raisins.

Serve as main dish, or second course, with no side dishes.

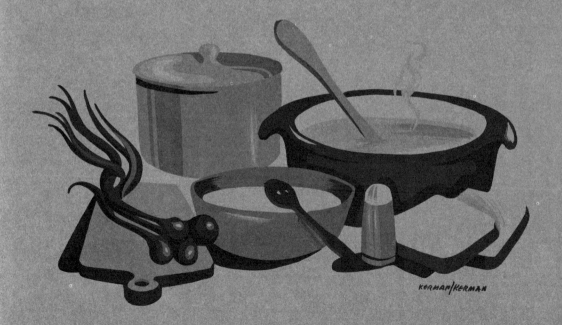

KERMAN/KERMAN

Soups & Drinks

41   MARAK BAGDAD

SOUP OF BAGDAD

Giblet soup

TRADITIONAL for Iraqi Jews

Preparing time: 20 minutes. Cooking time: 45 minutes. Serves 10

---

2 lbs. giblets (wings, gizzards, necks) • 2 cloves garlic, sliced • 2 celery leaves, chopped • 1 tbs. tomato juice • 2 medium potatoes, peeled and cubed • ½ lb. green peas, fresh or canned • 1 tbs. lemon juice • 1 small onion, chopped • 2 tbs. oil for frying • 10 cups hot water

---

Clean giblets and cut up. In a pan fry onion, add tomato juice and giblets, water, garlic, and vegetables (excluding peas). Bring to boil, reduce heat and cook over low heat for 30 mins. Add peas and continue to cook for additional 15 minutes. Remove from heat, and add lemon juice.
Serve with boiled rice or soup noodles.

42   MARAK YERAKOT MASORTI

BOBEH'S SURPRISE

Vegetable soup with beans and goose

TRADITIONAL

Preparing time: 15-20 mins. Cooking time: 1¼ hours. **Serves 6**

---

2 cups white (or navy) beans • 1 celery root, sliced • 1 small cauliflower • 4 potatoes, peeled and cubed • 2 carrots, diced • 10 ozs. vermicelli • 7 ozs. smoked goose (turkey may be substituted) • 2 cloves garlic • Basil • Parsley, chopped • Salt • Pepper

---

Place beans in a medium saucepan with water, and boil until soft. Add flowerets of cauliflower, potatoes, carrots, celery root. Continue to cook over low heat for another hour.
After this, add vermicelli, garlic, smoked goose, basil and parsley. Stir well, adding salt and pepper to taste. Continue to cook for another 15 minutes.
Serve hot, with crackers.

43   MARAK CHEMDAT HAARETZ

SABRA SOUP

Vegetable soup

NEW

Preparing time: 15 minutes. Cooking time: 45 minutes. **Serves 6**

Fresh vegetables, in season (about 12 ozs.) • 1 chicken bouillon cube • 6 cups water • Margarine • 1 tbs. parsley, chopped • Salt • Pepper

---

Peel vegetables, and cube. Stir them in a little margarine, add water and simmer over medium heat for 45 minutes. During cooking, add seasoning and bouillon cube.
Serve hot, garnished with chopped parsley, or dill.

44   MARAK TEIMANI

SPICY MEAT SOUP

TRADITIONAL for Yemenite Jews

Preparing time: 10 minutes. Cooking time: 45 minutes. Serves 5

1 lb. beef • 1 tbs. celery leaves, chopped • 5 cloves garlic • ¼ tsp. black pepper • 2 tomatoes, peeled and cubed • 3 whole cardamons • Salt • 1 tbs. parsley, chopped • 2 tbs. oil for frying • Coriander • 6 cups water

Cook meat in water about 30 minutes. Remove meat, and set aside the stock. In oil fry the garlic, coriander, celery leaves, parsley and tomatoes. Add to stock. Season with salt, pepper, and add cardamons. Stir and continue to cook for another 15 minutes.

45   MARAK HORPI B'NUSACH YEHUDAY TRIPOLI

WINTER SOUP

Smoked goose soup with vegetables

TRADITIONAL for Tripolitanian Jews

Preparing time: 30 minutes. Cooking time: 3 hours. Serves 6

---

3 ozs. smoked goose (turkey may be substituted) • 2 - 3 potatoes, sliced • 4 carrots, cubed • 7 ozs. pumpkin, cubed • 5 ozs. white (or navy) beans • 2 - 3 celery leaves, chopped • 1 chicken-soup cube • 1 onion, finely chopped • Oil for frying • 2 cloves garlic, minced • 1 tbs. ketchup • 3 pints water

---

Soak beans in water for 12 hours. Cook beans on high heat, until tender. Set aside.
In a little oil sauté goose with garlic and onion. Add all vegetables, and stew for 10 minutes.
Transfer to deep saucepan. Add water, the soup cube and ketchup, and mix well. Cover, and continue to simmer over medium heat for another hour. Add the beans shortly before serving.
Serve hot in soup plates, with croutons.

46   BORSCHT DRINK

COLD BEET JUICE

TRADITIONAL

Preparing time: 15-20 minutes. Cooking time 1½ hours. Serves 6

---

12 beets, peeled and grated • 1 onion, grated • 3 eggs • 1 cup sour cream • 4 tbs. sugar • ⅓ cup lemon juice • 6 pints water • 2 tsp. salt

---

Put beets, onion and salt in a pot of water. Cook over low heat for an hour and ten minutes.
Mix lemon and sugar together, and add to beets. Leave about 15 minutes to blend. Remove from heat. Beat eggs in a large

bowl. Slowly add the beets, stirring all the time to make sure it doesn't curdle. Cool, and chill in refrigerator. If desired serve with a spoonful of sour cream in each portion.
Serve cold, in tall glasses, as first course.
See photograph on page 75.

47 MARAK OFF CHAMATZMATZ

SOUR SOUP

Chicken soup and vegetables

TRADITIONAL for Greek Jews

Preparing time: 15 minutes. Cooking time: 20 minutes. Serves 8

---

2 lbs. whole chicken • 8 cups water • Juice of 1 lemon •
1 flat tsp. corn • Soup vegetables (carrots, onions, celery,
parsley) • 3 egg yolks • 1 cup soup noodles • Salt
• Pepper

Put whole chicken, with vegetables, into a large saucepan. Add 8 cups water, salt and pepper. (Note: to keep soup clear, tie parsley and celery leaves together.) Bring to a boil, continue to cook for 20 minutes, remove from heat, and strain. In a large Pyrex bowl prepare a smooth mixture of the egg yolks, cornmeal and lemon juice. When mixture is smooth, slowly add spoonfuls of the hot soup, stirring constantly.
Serve with soup almonds.

48 MARAK TIVONI

VEGETARIAN SOUP

Cold vegetable soup

TRADITIONAL for Spanish Jews

Preparing time: 20 minutes. Serves 8

---

4 tomatoes • 1 green pepper • 1 cucumber • 1 summer squash • 1 sweet red pepper • 1 tbs. parsley, chopped • 4 spring onions • 2 cloves garlic • 1 tbs. lemon juice • 1 chicken bouillon cube • 2 tsp. sugar • 1 tsp. salt • Pinch of hot red pepper • Pinch of black pepper

---

Wash and peel all vegetables (pour boiling water over tomatoes to remove skins). Cut into cubes, and place gradually into electric blender. After each cup of vegetables, add ¼ cup of water, blending continuously.
Add the bouillon cube, lemon juice, sugar and spices. Continue to blend for another 2 minutes.
Transfer the soup into a tall pitcher, and place in refrigerator for 5 - 6 hours. Serve very cold, in tall glasses.

49 MARAK SHUM

GARLIC SOUP

Soup with garlic and tomato purée

TRADITIONAL for Jews of India

Preparing time: 20 minutes. Cooking time: 20 minutes. Serves 5

---

7 ozs. tomato purée • 6 cups water • 4 tbs. oil for frying • 3 tbs. flour • Small head of garlic • Salt • Pepper

---

In a deep saucepan heat 3 tbs. oil. Stir in flour, and fry until light brown. Add 1 cup water, stirring constantly to prevent lumping. Gradually add rest of water and tomato purée, stirring constantly. When soup reaches boiling point, season with salt and pepper, and reduce heat. Continue to simmer for 15 mins.

Meanwhile heat the remaining 1 tbs. oil in a frying pan. Cut garlic into slices, and fry for half a minute, until golden. Add garlic to soup, and cook for another 5 minutes.
Serve hot, with croutons.

50   CHAMITZAH BORSHT

BORSCHT SOUP

Meat and beet soup

TRADITIONAL for Ukranian Jews

Preparing time: 20 minutes. Cooking time: 2 hours. Serves: 8-10

---

1 lb. beef, cubed • 1 lb. bones • 1 lb. beets • 1 large onion • 1 lb. cabbage, shredded • 4 large tomatoes • 3 ozs. tomato purée • 3 large potatoes, peeled • 1 tbs. sugar • Juice of 1 lemon • Salt • Pepper

---

In a saucepan pour 10 cups of water. Place in meat, bones, beets, onion and tomatoes mashed on rough grater, shredded cabbage, salt and pepper. Bring to boil on high heat. Reduce heat when boiling point is reached, and cook for 1½ hours, with lid on.
Put in whole potatoes, tomato purée, and cook for another half hour.
Before serving, add lemon juice and sugar. Stir well. (This nourishing soup is eaten by Russian Jews mainly during the severe winters, as often as twice a day).

51   KARPASIA

KNEIDEL SOUP, WITH CELERY

TRADITIONAL for Pesach

Preparing time: 30 minutes. Cooking time: 2 hours. Serves: 8-10

> 1 lb. beef, sliced • 1 - 2 bones • 2 tbs. ground beef •
> 1 cup matzo meal • 1 large onion • 3 cloves garlic •
> 1 large summer squash, sliced thinly • 2 tbs. celery,
> chopped • Parsley, chopped • 1 tsp. oil • 1 egg • Juice
> of 1 lemon • Black pepper • Salt

In a saucepan place bones, onion, meat, garlic, most of the
celery, parsley and squash. Add 4 cups water and let simmer
over low heat. Stew until liquid evaporates and meat is cooked.
Add six cups water, and continue to simmer over very low heat
with lid on for 1½ hours.
Combine matzo meal with ½ cup lukewarm water, oil and
ground beef. Mix well, to an even texture. Add remainder of
chopped celery and egg, and continue to mix.
Form one-inch balls. Drop them into soup and let cook for
20 minutes. Add seasoning to taste. Shortly before end of
cooking, add lemon juice.
Serve hot with matzos or crackers.

52   MARAK GOULASCH HUNGARI

HUNGARIAN GOULASH SOUP

Meat soup with dumplings

TRADITIONAL for Hungarian Jews

Preparing time: 30 minutes. Cooking time: 1 hour. Serves 8

½ lb. beef, cubed • 5 slices salami • 3 vienna sausages • ¼ cup chicken meat, cubed • ¼ cup oil for frying • 3 medium carrots, grated • 2 large onions, chopped • 4 large potatoes, peeled and cubed • 1 large tomato, peeled and chopped • 1 celery root, grated • 1 small parsley root, grated • 1 green pepper, cubed • 1 sweet red pepper, cubed • ½ tsp. chili powder • 8 cups water

In a large saucepan sauté onion in oil until golden. Add salami, beef, chicken, sausages and chili powder, and fry for another 10 minutes. Add 4 cups water, and cook over low heat. Add vegetables, except potatoes, to saucepan, plus the remaining 4 cups of water. Add seasoning, and continue to cook. About 20 minutes before dish is ready, add potatoes.

DUMPLINGS

½ cup flour • 1 egg • 2 tbs. water • Salt

Combine flour, egg, water and pinch of salt, and mix into a dough. Dough should be firm so it can be grated on a rough grater, into the boiling soup. Cook for 5 mins. This soup can be kept in the refrigerator for a few days. It is excellent for serving on cold winter days.

53   KREPLACH

DOUGH POCKETS, STUFFED WITH MEAT

TRADITIONAL for Polish Jews

Preparing time: 30-35 mins. Cooking time: 30 mins. Serves: 6-8

> 2 cups flour • 2 eggs, beaten • 1 lb. cooked ground meat • Clear soup (ready) • 2 tbs. cold water • ½ tsp. salt

Sift flour, adding salt. Slowly add eggs and water, and mix carefully to form a dough. Knead dough well, and roll to one-eighth inch thickness. Cut into 2½ inch squares. Place 1 tsp. cooked ground meat on each square. Pinch edges together, then drop into boiling soup and leave for at least 5 minutes. Serve 2 - 3 per portion.

54   KUFTA'OT MARAK PESACH

KNEIDAL SOUP

Matzo-meal balls in soup

TRADITIONAL

Preparing time: 25 mins. Cooking time: 10-12 mins. Serves: 6 - 8

> 3 eggs • 3½ cups matzo meal • ½ chicken bouillon cube • 1 tsp. celery leaves, chopped • Nutmeg • Juice of ½ lemon • Salt • Pepper

Beat eggs well, adding bouillon cube, salt, pepper and pinch of nutmeg. Add lemon juice and celery leaves. Continue to beat. Slowly add matzo meal, using a wooden spoon to stir. When matzo meal thickens knead by hand. After the matzo meal has been thoroughly kneaded, form small balls (1 inch). Arrange in deep dish and leave in refrigerator for at least three hours. Prepare a clear chicken soup, and when it reaches boiling point, drop in matzo balls. Leave for 10 - 12 minutes.
Serve 3 - 4 balls per bowl of soup. Add lemon juice to taste.

55   MARAK UFOONA BAYTI
PEA SOUP

TRADITIONAL for European Jews

Preparing time: 15 minutes. Cooking time: 3½ hours. Serves 6

---

3 lbs. beef cut to cubes • 3 carrots, diced • 1 onion, diced • 1½ cups split peas • ½ tsp. celery salt • 10 cups water • Salt • Pepper

---

Brown the beef and onions. Place peas in large pot, in water. Cook on low heat for 1 hour, then bring to boil, adding beef, onions, carrots, and seasoning. Cover and cook on low heat for about 2½ hours. Place meat on a plate. Press the soup through a sieve, and transfer to a soup tureen. When serving, see that each portion of soup contains several pieces of meat.

56   DAHL GOUSH
LENTIL AND MEAT SOUP

TRADITIONAL for Jews of India

Preparing time: 20 minutes. Cooking time: 1½ hours. Serves 8

---

1 cup lentils • 1 lb. beef • 8 cups water • 1 large onion, chopped • 3 ozs. tomato purée • ¼ cup oil for frying • 4 large potatoes, peeled • ½ tsp. saffron • Garlic powder • Black pepper • 1 tsp. cumin • 1 tsp. caraway seeds • Salt

---

Fry onion in oil. Add tomato purée and spices. Bring to boil while stirring. Add water and when boiling point is again reached place in meat and lentils. Cook for at least an hour over low heat. 20 minutes before dish is ready, add potatoes cut in halves.

Serve in soup bowls, adding half a potato and a portion of meat to each serving. If desired, the meat can be served separately as a main course, with side dishes.

KERMAN/KERMAN

Fish

57 MIMRACH DUG MALOO'ACH

SALTY SNACK

Herring and potato spread

NEW

Preparing time: 15 minutes. Cooking time: 30 minutes. Serves 6

---

3 herrings, filleted • ½ lb. potatoes • Parsley, chopped •
Black olives

Cook potatoes in saucepan with water. When soft, remove and
let cool. Mince together with herring. Mix well.
Garnish with chopped parsley, and black olives.
Serve as first course.

58   KRISTADA

FISH STEW IN EGGS

TRADITIONAL for Spanish Jews

Preparing time: 10 minutes. Cooking time: 10-15 mins. Serves 4

---

4 filleted fish (any freshwater fish, according to choice) •
2 eggs • Juice of 1 lemon • 5 cloves garlic, minced •
1 tbs. parsley, chopped • 1 tsp. celery, chopped • Oil for
frying • Salt • ½ cup water

Fry fish in deep oil, until golden in color. Remove and place
in a shallow pan.
In a second pan put 1 tbs. oil, and heat. Add beaten eggs. Stir
until set, and add lemon juice, salt to taste, garlic, parsley
and celery. Mix, and pour over fried fish. Add water, and
simmer over low heat until liquid evaporates.
Serve hot, as main course, with pernod.

59   DUG B'NUSACH YEHUDAY TRIPOLI

FISH TRIPOLI

Grouper cooked with potatoes and spices

TRADITIONAL for Tripolitanian Jews

Preparing time: 25 minutes. Cooking time: 30-40 mins. Serves 6

---

6 slices grouper (5 ozs. each) • 2 lbs. potatoes, peeled
and sliced • Spring onion, chopped • Parsley, chopped •
6 anchovies, filleted • ½ cup oil for frying • 1 clove
garlic. minced • Salt • Pepper

Clean fish slices, removing skin and bone. Rinse well, and dry in paper towel. Sprinkle with salt and pepper, and set aside. Arrange ½ quantity of finely sliced potatoes in thinly-oiled baking dish. Add salt and pepper to taste. On top of potatoes sprinkle onion, garlic and parsley.

Place fish slices in a baking dish. Top each one with anchovy fillet. Cover fish with remainder of potatoes, and sprinkle on oil, and salt. Bake in a moderate oven for 30 - 40 minutes, checking occasionally. Remove and let cool.

Before serving reheat either in oven or on a hotplate.

Serve hot, with wines or cool drinks.

60   DUG BURI B'NUSACH AMAMI

FRIED MACKEREL

Fried fish

TRADITIONAL

Preparing time: 20 minutes. Cooking time: 20 minutes. Serves 6

3 lbs. small mackerel • Chopped parsley • Juice of 1 lemon • 1 clove garlic • Oil for frying • Salt • Pepper

Clean fish properly, and dry in paper towel. Fry in hot oil, in saucepan, over medium heat. Add garlic, parsley, salt and pepper to taste. Turn fish twice on each side during frying. Add lemon juice when fish is ready.

Serve hot as main dish, with white wine.

61   DUG ROSH HANIKRA

WHITE GROTTO FISH

Spicy fish dish

NEW

Preparing time: 15 minutes. Cooking time: 30 minutes. Serves 6

> 2 fish, about 1¼ lbs. each (any freshwater fish, according
> to choice) • 2 tomatoes • 1 tsp. fresh hot pepper •
> Margarine • Juice of 1 lemon • 2 tbs. ketchup • Salt •
> Pepper • ½ cup water

Clean fish well, slice into portions, sprinkle on salt and pepper,
and place in a greased baking dish.
Pour boiling water over tomatoes, remove peel, and chop.
Mix tomatoes with ketchup and hot pepper, and pour over fish.
Add ½ cup water, lemon juice and bake in oven for 25 minutes.
Serve as main course, with boiled vegetables and vin rosé.

62   DUG GRUZIA

RUSSIAN CARP

TRADITIONAL for Russian Jews

Preparing time: 35 minutes. Cooking time: 50 minutes. Serves 6

> 3 lbs. sliced carp • Celery leaves, chopped • 6 tbs.
> prepared horseradish • 3 sour apples • 2 onions, chopped
> • Saffron • Parsley, chopped • 1 tbs. lemon juice • 2 tsp.
> vinegar • Salt • 2 bayleaves • Pepper • 6 slices lemon
> • ½ tsp. sugar

Place the celery leaves, parsley and onion in a pan. Add 5
cups of water. Cook for 15-20 minutes. Add vinegar, bay leaves,

pinch of saffron, and carp slices to pan, and cook over low heat for 25-30 minutes. Bake apples, and mash. Blend with horseradish, 1 tsp. water, lemon juice and ½ tsp. sugar.
Remove fish from pan and grill each side for 5 minutes. Arrange on flat plates, pour 1 tbs. of liquid in pan over fish. Decorate with lemon slices. Horseradish mixture can be served separately, or topped on each slice.
Serve as first or main course.

63 KUDOOREI GEFILTE FISH

GEFILTE FISH BALLS

Stuffed fish balls

TRADITIONAL

Preparing time: 40 minutes. Cooking time: 2½ hours. Serves 6

> Whole whitefish (3 lbs.) • 2 eggs • 2 onions chopped •
> 3 carrots, sliced lengthwise • 2 tbs. matzo meal • Lemon
> • Parsley • ½ tsp. sugar • ½ cup ice water • 1½ qts.
> water • Pepper • Salt

Place bones and head of fish in a pot with 3 pints of water, salt and pepper to taste, and boil over medium heat. Prepare remainder of fish, grind it and add chopped onion. Carefully add eggs, sugar, matzo meal, ice water, salt and pepper. Chop the mixture very finely. Shape into balls.
Reduce to low heat the pot containing bones and head, gradually put in the fish balls, add the carrots, and cook for two hours. Season to taste, and cook for another ½ hour. Discard head, bones and water. Cool fish, balls and arrange on a serving dish. Garnish with lemon and parsley.

64   DUG B'MITZ HADARIM

FISH IN ORANGE JUICE

NEW

Preparing time: 15 minutes. Cooking time: 30 minutes. Serves 6

---

1 lb. 10 ozs. hake, or grouper • **1 cup natural orange juice** • Flour • 6-12 orange slices • **Corn starch** • **Salt** • Oil for frying

---

Clean fish thoroughly. Coat in flour and fry in oil. Place in a baking dish, and let cool.
Bring orange juice to a boil, thicken with some cornstarch, and pour over cool fish.
Serve cold, decorated with orange slices, as a main course.
Serve with boiled potatoes, carrots, cauliflower and squash, with white wine.

65   GEFILTE FISH

STUFFED CARP, WITH ALMOND FLAVOR

TRADITIONAL for Polish Jews

Preparing time: 30 minutes. Cooking time: 1½ hours. Serves 8

---

2 lbs. carp. • 1 large onion, sliced • 2 eggs • 1 slice white bread, soaked in water and drained • 1 heaped tbs. matzo meal or bread crumbs • 1 tbs. almonds, shelled and chopped • 2 tbs. water • 1 tbs. oil for frying • 1 tsp. sugar • 1 hard-boiled egg • Salt • Pepper

---

Clean fish well, and slice. With a sharp knife remove the meat, leaving the skins intact. Place skins on a plate, and set

aside. Sauté onion in a little oil. Mince fish meat together with soaked bread, almonds, fried onion and hard-boiled egg. In a bowl combine minced fish, 2 eggs, 2 tbs. water, bread crumbs, salt, pepper and 1 tsp. sugar. Mix well.
Stuff the skin with fish mixture. Place in the boiling stock, cover, and simmer over low heat for 1½ hours.

STOCK

> 1 large onion, sliced • 1 parsley root • 2 carrots, peeled and sliced • 5 cups water • ½ tsp. sugar • Salt • Pepper

Bring to boil water, vegetables and seasoning. Place stuffed fish in saucepan and cook (as above). Let cool, and then remove stuffed fish carefully from saucepan. Place on an oval serving dish. Strain stock, and decorate fish with slices of carrots. This is a Friday evening — pre-Sabbath — dish for Eastern Jewry. It is served with vodka or brandy.
See photograph on page 85.

66   MA'AFEH DUGIM

SPICED FISH DISH

Baked fish in tomato sauce

TRADITIONAL among Greek Jews

Preparing time: 30 minutes. Cooking time: 45 minutes. Serves 5

> 2 lbs. sea fish (any available) • 1 large tomato, sliced • 2 tbs. tomato purée • ½ cup dry white wine • ½ cup oil • 1 tbs. parsley, chopped • Juice of 1 lemon • 1 medium onion, chopped • 1 large clove garlic, minced • 2 bay leaves • Salt • Pepper

Clean the fish, and cut into slices. Sprinkle with some salt, and a few drops of lemon juice. Leave fish to stand for ½ hour. Arrange fish slices in a baking dish. Put over onion, garlic seasoning and bay leaves. Place a tomato slice on each slice of fish.

In a bowl blend tomato purée, oil, wine, remainder of lemon juice, parsley, salt and pepper. Add some water if necessary. Pour this mixture over the fish.

Cover with aluminium foil and bake in a moderate oven for 30-45 minutes.

Serve as a main course with white or sparkling wine.

67   DUG YAFFO

JONAH'S FISH

Fish in white sauce

NEW

Preparing time: 15 minutes. Cooking time: 20 minutes. Serves 5

---

1 lb. hake, or filleted fish • 1 medium onion, sliced • ½ cup vinegar • 2 cups water • 5 bay leaves • 5 peppercorns • 1 carrot, peeled and sliced • ½ tsp. flour • 1 egg yolk • 2 tbs. milk • 1 tsp. sugar • Salt

---

Sprinkle fish with salt, and set aside for ½ hour.

In a saucepan combine water, vinegar, ½ the carrot, onion, bay leaves, peppercorns and sugar and cook for 10 minutes.

Rinse fish, add to saucepan, and cook for 10 minutes more. Make a batter of egg yolk, milk and flour. Add to fish, stirring constantly. Bring to boil until sauce thickens. Set aside to cool.

Place fish in a glass bowl. Pour over white sauce, and decorate with carrot slices.

Serve as main course, with baked potatoes, glazed carrots and white wine.

68   BAKALA SFARADI

SPICED HAKE

TRADITIONAL for Spanish Jews

Preparing time: 20 minutes. Cooking time: 35 minutes. Serves 6

---

2 lbs. hake (or other filleted fish) • 4 large tomatoes, sliced • 1 tbs. parsley, chopped • 1 medium clove of garlic, minced • ½ cup oil for frying • 2½ cups water • 2 tbs. vinegar • ½ tsp. saffron • ½ tsp. paprika • Salt • Pepper

---

Cut fish into slices, and wash. Sprinkle with salt and vinegar, and let marinate for 15 minutes.
In a shallow saucepan put ¼ cup oil, half the tomato slices, a little parsley, and garlic. Wipe off excess salt from fish.
Pour over mixture in saucepan, and sprinkle with black pepper to taste. Fry for 5 minutes, add remainder of oil, tomatoes, 1 cup water, and continues to cook. When boiling point is reached, add 1½ cups water, the paprika and saffron. Reduce heat and continue to simmer for 20 minutes more, or until fish is ready. Serve fish hot, in sauce, as a main dish, with brandy or white wine.

69   FILLET DUG SANDAL

SANDAL SOLE

Sole in techina sauce

NEW

Preparing time: 10 minutes. Cooking time: 20 minutes. Serves 6

---

3 medium soles • 3 ozs. smoked salmon • 1 tin techina sauce • 1 hard-boiled egg • 2 cloves garlic, minced • Juice of 1 lemon • 1 tbs. parsley, chopped • Salt • Pepper

---

Remove fish bone carefully. Cut filleted fish into slices, and set aside. Mince smoked salmon and hard-boiled egg. Mix well, and spread over filleted fish slices, and roll. Fasten each roll with a toothpick, or tie with thread. Place in a baking dish and bake for 20 minutes in a moderate oven. Remove and let cool. In a bowl combine techina sauce, lemon juice, salt & pepper to taste, garlic and a little water. Blend into a smooth sauce, and pour over cooled fish rolls.
Serve cold, garnished with chopped parsley, as first course.

70 DAG B'ROTEV CHARIF

SPICED FISH IN TOMATO SAUCE

TRADITIONAL for Turkish Jews

Preparing time: 20 minutes. Cooking time: 45 minutes. Serves 5

---

2 lbs. fish (according to choice) • 1 large onion, chopped • 1 tsp. chili powder • ½ cup oil for frying • 1 small garlic, crushed • 7 ozs. tomato purée • ½ tsp. cinnamon • ¼ tsp. ground cumin • ½ tsp. ground caraway seeds • 2 level tsp. sugar • 1 green pepper, whole • 2 cups water • Salt

---

Wash fish and sprinkle with salt. Set aside.
Sauté onion in oil, garlic, chili powder and ½ cup water. Simmer, and stir continuously. Add tomato purée, sugar, seasoning and another ½ cup water. Continue to simmer over low heat until gravy is smooth and thick.
Add remainder of water, green pepper and fish. Cover well and cook for 30 minutes longer, or until fish is tender. If liquid evaporates, add a little water during cooking.
Serve as first course, with white wine.
See photograph on page 46.

71   DUGIM B'LIMON

FISH STEW IN LEMON JUICE

TRADITIONAL

Preparing time: 10 minutes. Cooking time: 60 minutes. Serves 4

4 filleted fish (any sea fish, according to choice) •
6 cloves garlic • Juice of 1 lemon • 1 artichoke stalk,
peeled and sliced • 1 tbs. celery, chopped • 1 tbs.
parsley, chopped • ½ tsp. red pepper • Salt • 1 cup
water • Oil for frying

Sauté garlic in a little oil in a saucepan, until golden. Add
red pepper, water, parsley, artichoke stalk, fish and salt. Cook
over low heat for 1 hour. Before removing fish from heat add
lemon juice, and continue to cook until a thick sauce forms
at the bottom of the saucepan.
Serve hot, as main course, with white wine.

KERMAN/KERMAN

Poultry

72   OFF HAAVIV

SPRING CHICKEN

Chicken with peel of eggplants, peppers and tomatoes

NEW

Preparing time: 15 minutes. Cooking time: 1½ hours. Serves 6

---

1 chicken (3 lbs.) • 2 large eggplants • 4 tomatoes •
½ tsp. chili powder • 5 cloves garlic, minced • Chopped
parsley • 6 green peppers • 1 onion, chopped • Oil for
frying • Salt

Cut the chicken into 8 portions, and fry in oil until golden.
Put aside. Pour boiling water over tomatoes, remove skin and
slice. Cut peppers into long, narrow strips, peel eggplants
and cut peels into small strips.
In hot oil quick-fry onion, garlic and parsley. Mix chili powder
with some water, add to saucepan. When some of the liquid
evaporates, add chicken and continue cooking for 10 minutes,
turning occasionally. Add salt to taste.
Place strips of eggplant peel on chicken, repeat with peppers,
and cover with tomatoes. Springle salt over, place lid tightly
on saucepan, and let cook on very low heat for an hour. Shake
saucepan occasionally during cooking.
Serve hot as main dish.

73 OFF MEMULAH B'ROTEV TAPOOZIM

STUFFED CHICKEN IN ORANGE SAUCE

NEW

Preparing time: 30 minutes. Cooking time: 30-40 mins. Serves 4

> 2 lbs. chicken, whole • 1 cup dry white wine • 5 cloves garlic, minced • 2 bay leaves • 1½ cups water • ½ cup orange juice • Pinch of nutmeg • 1 carrot, peeled and sliced • ½ tsp. flour • Oil for frying • 1 orange, sliced into moons • Salt • Pepper • 2 celery leaves, chopped

STUFFING

> 2 chicken livers • 1 egg • 3 tbs. oil for frying • 3 tbs. matzo meal • 1 small onion, chopped • 1 tbs. parsley, chopped • Salt • Pepper

To make stuffing, fry livers and onion in oil over low heat. Mince the fried liver and onion together, place in a bowl with matzo meal, parsley, egg, salt and pepper, and mix well. Stuff chicken with this mixture.

In a shallow saucepan fry chicken on all sides. Rub mixture of minced garlic, salt and pepper over chicken.

Place in a baking dish, add water and wine, top with carrots, celery, nutmeg and bay leaves. Bake in a moderate oven for 30 minutes, basting occasionally.

Remove chicken from oven. Blend flour and orange juice, pour into baking dish, return chicken to oven, and continue to bake for another 10 minutes.

Cut into four portions and decorate each with an orange slice. Serve as main course, with white wine or rosé.

See photograph on page 86.

74 OFF B'YAYIN V'ZAYTAIM — NUSACH MOROCCO

CHICKEN MOROCCO

Chicken and black olives cooked in wine

TRADITIONAL for Moroccan Jews

Preparing time: 25 minutes. Cooking time: 45 minutes. Serves 6

> 1 chicken (2 lbs.) • 40 pitted black olives (20 finely chopped) • 2 tbs. wine vinegar • ½ glass white wine • 3 tbs. oil for frying • 3 cloves garlic (whole) • Salt • Pepper

Cut chicken into 8 portions. Put a little oil in saucepan, and fry garlic on medium heat. When oil is hot, add chicken, salt and pepper to taste. Continue to fry until chicken is golden-brown. Add wine vinegar and olives to saucepan. As vinegar evaporates, add the white wine and as wine evaporates add a little water. When boiling point is reached, reduce heat. Continue to cook for a time, until most of the liquid has evaporated, and chicken is tender.
Serve as main dish with boiled potatoes or asparagus.

75 YONUT HASHALOM

PIGEONS OF PEACE

Stewed pigeons in wine

NEW

Preparing time: 20 minutes. Cooking time: 1½ hours. Serves 6

> 5 whole, medium pigeons cleaned (squabs or cornish hens may be substituted) • 1 onion, chopped • 2 tbs. parsley, chopped • 1 tbs. celery, chopped • 4 cloves garlic, crushed • 6 bay leaves • ¾ glass white wine • 2 tbs. margarine • Salt • Pepper • Oil for frying

Divide pigeons in half, fry in oil until golden, and remove. Transfer remaining oil into saucepan, add margarine, and heat until hot. Add parsley, celery, garlic, onion, bayleaves and sauté for 2-3 minutes. Add the pigeons, fry for another 10 mins., sprinkle with some salt and pepper, and pour wine over. Continue to cook.
When the wine evaporates, add water to cover pigeons, and cover saucepan. Simmer over low heat for 1 hour.
Before serving place saucepan in medium oven for 2 minutes.
Serve as main dish, with white wine and baked potatoes.

76   TZAVAR HODU MISHPACHTI

STUFFED TURKEY NECK WITH NUTS

TRADITIONAL for Spanish Jews

Preparing time: 60 minutes. Cooking time: 60 minutes. Serves 8

> 8 turkey necks • 4 slices white bread, soaked in water and drained • 1 tbs. chicken fat • 3 ozs. walnuts, chopped • 2 tbs. parsley, chopped • 2 eggs • 1 medium onion, sliced • 2 tbs. oil for frying • 1 cup water • Salt • Pepper

Carefully remove and clean skin from neck of turkeys. Discard bones. In a bowl combine soaked bread and 1 egg. Mash with fork and mix. Add seasoning and nuts, second egg, chicken fat and mix.
Sew turkey necks skins on one end, and fill with stuffing, to three quarters full to allow for swelling during cooking. Sew other end closed, with needle and thread. Pour 1 cup boiling water over stuffed skins. Sauté onion in oil, add stuffed skins and fry on all sides for a few minutes. Add water, and cook over low heat for 45 minutes.
Remove stuffed skins and place in a greased baking dish. Bake for 15 minutes.
If desired, stuffed skins can be cooked together with roast meat.
Serve as first course or as a side dish to a main course with cooked carrots and sweet-sour cabbage.

77   SHOK OFF MEMULAH

SATURDAY'S

Chicken legs stuffed with chopped liver

NEW

Preparing time: 20 minutes. Cooking time: 60 minutes. Serves 6

6 chicken legs • ½ lb. chicken or beef liver • 1 onion,
finely chopped • 2 hard-boiled eggs • Oil for frying •
Salt • Pepper

With a sharp knife make a slit along the chicken legs, and
carefully remove bone.
Sauté onion and liver in oil. Remove and mince finely the fried
liver, onion and hard-boiled eggs. In a bowl combine liver
mixture, add a little oil and seasoning, and mix well. Stuff boned
legs with mixture, place the legs in a greased baking dish,
and bake in a moderate oven for an hour.
Serve as main course, with fried potatoes, glazed carrots or
stewed vegetables, and vin rosé.

78   KAVED OFF B'NUSACH YEHUDI

JEWISH STYLE CHICKEN LIVER

Chicken liver in wine sauce and mushrooms

TRADITIONAL for Lybian Jews

Preparing time: 15 minutes. Cooking time: 20 minutes. Serves 6

12 chicken livers • ½ cup mushrooms, fresh or tinned •
1 medium onion, finely chopped • 2 cloves garlic, crushed
• Oil for frying • 2 tbs. margarine • ½ cup red wine •
Salt • Pepper • Chicken stock

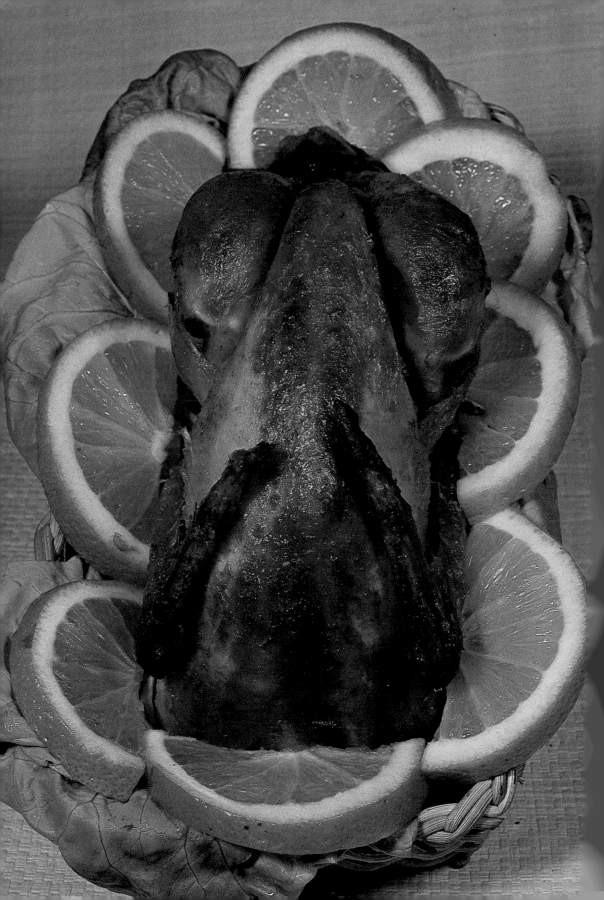

Heat oil and margarine in frying pan, add onion, garlic and liver, and fry.

Rinse mushrooms well, cut into fine slices, add to frying pan, and continue to fry. While frying pour in the wine. When it evaporates, add a little stock, salt and pepper to taste.

Serve hot as first or main course.

79   OFF B'AFARSEK

PEACH CHICK

Chicken breast with peaches

NEW

Preparing time: 30 minutes. Cooking time: 50 minutes. Serves 4

> 1 lb. chicken (or turkey) breast • 6 tbs. margarine •
> 1 onion, chopped • 4 peaches, not too ripe • 2 cups
> water • 2 tbs. lemon juice • 2 tbs. sugar • 1 chicken
> bouillon cube • ¼ tsp. paprika • Salt

Cut chicken into small cubes. Fry in saucepan, with 2 tbs. margarine. Add salt and paprika and continue to fry until golden brown. Sauté onion separately in 2 tbs. margarine, until golden. Place chicken in casserole dish. Sprinkle onion over, and cook over low heat.

Meanwhile slice washed peaches into rings, removing pits, and sauté in remainder of margarine. Arrange sliced peaches over onion in casserole. In a pan boil 2 cups water, add bouillon cube, sugar and lemon juice. Pour over meat and peaches, and continue to simmer for another 20 minutes.

Serve as main dish with spaghetti, rice or mashed potatoes.

80   KETSITSOT OFF

CHICKEN RISSOLES

Ground chicken balls

TRADITIONAL for Russian Jews

Preparing time: 20 minutes. Cooking time: 10 minutes. Serves 4

> 1 cooked chicken, finely ground • 1 onion, grated •
> Parsley • ½ tsp. sage • 4 eggs • 1 cup matzo meal •
> Oil for frying, or fat • Salt • Pepper

Mix chicken, onion, parsley, salt, pepper, sage, two eggs,
matzo meal, and form into balls by hand. Beat remaining two
eggs, dip the balls in beaten eggs. Heat oil or fat in frying pan,
when hot, drop in balls, and brown all over.
Serve as main course, with fresh salad.

81   CHAZEH HODU MEMULAH

TURKEY TREAT

Breast of turkey slices, stuffed with mushrooms

NEW

Preparing time: 20 minutes. Cooking time: 30 minutes. Serves 6

> 2 lbs. breast of turkey • 1 onion, finely chopped • Parsley,
> finely chopped • 2½ cups mushrooms, cubed • Salt
> • Pepper • Margarine • Oil for frying

Cut breast into 6 slices. Pound each slice well and set aside.
Sauté mushrooms in a little margarine, or stew with water,
and drain. Fry onion, parsley and mushrooms, stirring occasion-

ally. Add seasoning, and remove from heat. Divide mixture into six portions, place over each turkey slice, and roll. Fasten slice with toothpick or tie with thread.

Fry rolls in a little oil until golden on all sides. Remove to a greased baking dish, pour over a little water, and bake in a moderate oven for 25 minutes.

Serve as a main course with fried potatoes and stewed vegetables — cauliflower, squash or carrots.

82   OFF B'KARPAS

CALCUTTA CHICKEN

Chicken strips with celery

TRADITIONAL for Jews from India

Preparing time: 15 minutes. Cooking time: 15 mins. Serves: 6-8

> 2 lbs. chicken breast • 5 celery stalks, well chopped • 5 spring onions • 2 ozs. margarine • 2 tbs. soya sauce • 1 heaped tbs. brown sugar • 1 tbs. cornstarch • 2 tbs. water

Cut breast of chicken into strips. Fry in margarine on medium heat until brown. Add celery stalks and spring onions. Continue to fry for another 2-3 minutes while stirring. Add sugar, soya sauce, constarch (diluted in 2 tbs. water). Continue to stir on low heat, until thick and smooth gravy is formed.

Serve as a main course, with boiled rice.

83   SALAT OFF

CUBED CHICKEN IN KETCHUP

NEW

Preparing time: 10 minutes. Cooking time: 20 minutes. Serves 6

---

14 ozs. chicken breast • Ketchup • Salt • Pepper • Black or stuffed olives

---

Cook chicken in saucepan with water to cover and seasoning. When tender remove from saucepan and let cool. Cut chicken into cubes or strips, add 2 tbs. ketchup, and mix slowly in order to preserve the shape of the cubes.
Serve cold, as first course. Decorate with black or stuffed olives.

84   MANAH PNIMI'OT NUSACH YEHUDAI TURKIAH

TURKISH TASTE

Gizzards with vegetables

TRADITIONAL for Turkish Jews

Preparing time: 20 minutes. Cooking time: 45 minutes. Serves 6

---

18 chicken gizzards • 1 large onion, finely chopped • 1 tomato, mashed • 1 carrot sliced • Marjoram • 3 cloves garlic, crushed • ½ glass red wine • Oil for frying • Margarine • Salt • Pepper·

Clean gizzards well. Boil them in water until almost done. In saucepan heat oil and a little margarine. Add onion, carrot

and garlic, and sauté until golden.
Add the gizzards, continue to fry for 15 minutes, stirring occasionally. Add seasoning, while stirring. Pour in wine, and continue to fry until this evaporates. Add tomato, stir, reduce heat and cover. Simmer for 25 minutes, stirring occasionally. The dish is ready when the sauce has thickened and the gizzards are brown.
Serve hot as first or main course.

85   CHAZEH HODU B'ROTEV YAYIN

TURKEY BREAST IN WHITE WINE

NEW

Preparing time: 10 minutes. Cooking time: 20 minutes. Serves 6

> 2 lbs. meat from breast of turkey • ½ bottle white wine •
> Flour • Oil for frying

Cut turkey breast into 6 slices. Coat in flour and fry for 2 mins. Arrange fried slices in greased baking dish, add wine, and bake in oven for 15 minutes.
Serve hot as main course, with roast potatoes and vegetables.

86   PILLAO

RICE WITH CHICKEN AND CARROTS

TRADITIONAL for Bukhara Jews

Preparing time: 15 minutes. Cooking time: 45 minutes. Serves 6

---

1 lb. chicken meat, cubed • 3 large carrots, shredded •
2 large onions, sliced • ¼ cup oil for frying • 1 cup rice
• 2 cups water • Salt • Pepper

In hot oil brown onion and carrots. Add cubed chicken, stir
well, and cook for 10 minutes over low heat. Add boiling water
and season, stir and add the rice. Wrap a towel around the
lid, and cover saucepan tightly. Cook for 30 minutes on low
heat, without stirring.
Serve hot on flat plates.

87   CHAMIN HODU

TURKEY CUBES

Turkey meat balls in tomato sauce

TRADITIONAL for Jews of India

Preparing time: 15 minutes. Cooking time: 50 mins. Serves: 5-6

---

2 lbs. turkey meat • ¼ cup oil for frying • 4 cloves garlic,
minced • 3 cups potatoes, peeled and cubed • 1½ cups
water • ½ tsp. saffron • 1 large onion, sliced • Salt
• Pepper

Cut turkey meat into cubes. In a shallow pan brown meat and
onion, in oil. Add water, garlic, salt and pepper, and cook
over low heat for 15 minutes.
Add potatoes and saffron to meat. Continue to simmer for
additional 20 minutes.
Serve as main course, without side dishes.

KERMAN/KERMAN

Meat

88 UMTSAT EGEL B'NUSACH KAFRIM

COUNTRY STEAK

Veal steak with artichokes

NEW

Preparing time: 15 minutes. Cooking time: 45 minutes Serves 6

---

6 veal steaks • 2 artichokes • 4 potatoes, sliced • Juice
of 1 lemon • 4 tbs. oil • Margarine • Salt • Pepper

Beat steaks with a knife handle. In a pan fry steaks in a little
margarine, and sprinkle on salt.
Grease Pyrex or baking dish with margarine, place half quantity
of potatoes in baking dish. Sprinkle on salt and pepper to taste.
Lay fried steaks on top of the potatoes. Add some water to
the gravy left in the pan, and pour this over steaks.
Remove leaves and chokes of artichokes, cut hearts into
medium slices, and leave to soak in a bowl with lemon juice
for 10 minutes. Remove, and place on steaks, with remaining
potatoes and a few drops of oil. Sprinkle with salt, and bake
in moderate oven for ½ hour.
Serve in baking dish, dividing into portions while hot.

89 SHIZIFIADAH

PRUNELLA

Cooked meat with prunes

TRADITIONAL for Litvakian Jews

Preparing time: 20 minutes. Cooking time: 60 minutes. Serves 4

> 1 lb. beef • 1 lb. prunes • 3 ozs. margarine • 1 onion, sliced • 2 tbs. sugar • 2 cups water • Pinch of nutmeg • ¼ tsp. cinnamon • 1 tsp. pepper • Salt

Cut the meat into cubes. Heat margarine in a shallow pan, place in meat, onion, salt, pepper and cook over low heat until meat is browned. Add water, and cover pan. Let simmer for another 30 minutes. About 10 minutes before dish is cooked, add prunes, sugar, nutmeg and cinnamon.
Serve as a main dish, with rice, macaroni or potatoes.

90 KADUREY ITLIZ HAMISHPACHA

ITLIZ'S

Veal or turkey meat rissoles, in white sauce

NEW

Preparing time: 10 minutes. Cooking time: 25 minutes. Serves 6

> 1½ lbs. veal or turkey meat, minced • 1 cup white wine • ½ cup margarine • 5 tbs. flour • 1 chicken bouillon cube • 1 cup water • 2 eggs • Salt • Pepper

In a bowl combine meat, eggs, salt and pepper. Mix well, and form into balls. Arrange in a baking dish.

In a pan melt margarine, and while stirring add flour, bouillon cube, wine and water. Let simmer over low heat for 10 mins., stirring constantly.

Remove from heat, strain and pour over meatballs. Bake in a moderate oven for 20 minutes.

Serve as main course, with rice and cooked vegetables.

91   REGEL KRUSHAH

VEAL IN ASPIC

Meat veal leg, in aspic

TRADITIONAL

Preparing time: 20 minutes. Cooking time: 30 mins. Serves: 8-10

Medium leg of veal • 3 hard-boiled eggs • Parsley, chopped • 2 large carrots • Juice of 1 lemon • Black pepper • Salt

---

Cook the leg of veal in a pan, in 5 cups of water, together with carrots. Bring to boil over high heat. When boiling point is reached reduce to low heat, and cook for another 25-30 minutes, until meat is tender.

Remove leg from saucepan, separate meat from bone, and chop or mince meat.

Put meat in a Pyrex dish, or glass bowl. Slice carrots and eggs into moons, and place over meat. Sprinkle with a little parsley, salt and pepper to taste. Pour liquid from saucepan into the bowl and set aside to cool. Place in refrigerator overnight, allowing it to set.

Before serving, cut into squares and squeeze over lemon juice. Serve as first course with red wine and crackers. Decorate each portion with a slice of lemon.

92   KTSITSOT BASAR V'BURGUL

ORIENTAL SANDWICH

Meat balls with groats

TRADITIONAL for Syrian Jews

Preparing time: 40 minutes. Cooking time: 30-40 mins. Serves 6

½ lb. minced beef • 3 ozs. groats (or dry lentils) •
½ cup parsley, chopped • 1 large onion, grated • 3 cloves
garlic, crushed • Salt • Pepper • Oil for frying

Soak groats in cold water for 15 minutes, and drain. Put meat
into a bowl, add groats, parsley, garlic, onion, salt and pepper.
Mix well and let stand for 10 minutes. Form into oval shapes,
and fry in hot oil.
Serve with vegetable salad, adding some of the oil left over
from frying. If possible, serve inside pitta (hollow, flat bread).

93   BASAR ME'UDEH — NUSACH ILANA

ILANA'S MEAT RECIPE

Sliced stewed meat, with vegetables

NEW

Preparing time: 15 minutes. Cooking time: 1½-2 hours. Serves 6

---

2 lbs. sirloin of beef • 2 tomatoes, mashed, or 1 tin
tomatoe purée • 1 cup red wine • 2 ozs. margarine • 1
onion, minced • 3 cloves garlic • Oil for frying • Small
portion smoked goose (or turkey) • 1 beef bouillon cube •
6 celery leaves, cooked • Salt • Pepper

Slice meat thinly. Place a little oil and the margarine in a saucepan. Fry the onion, garlic and smoked goose for five minutes. Add the meat. Sprinkle with salt and pepper to taste. Continue to fry until golden. Add the wine, and cook over medium heat until it evaporates. Add mashed tomatoes or purée. Let liquid evaporate a little, then add ½ cup lukewarm water. Reduce heat to low, cover the saucepan and let simmer for 1½-2 hours. While cooking, add lukewarm water from time to time, when required. Towards the end of cooking, add bouillon cube and celery leaves.

Serve hot as main dish, with red or sparkling wine.

94   TSLI ZEITIM MAROKA'I

ROAST BEEF IN OLIVES

TRADITIONAL for Moroccan Jews

Preparing time: 25 minutes. Cooking time: 1½ hours. Serves 6

---

1 lb. thin-fat beef, cubed • ½ lb. green olives • 1 medium head of garlic, crushed • 8-10 celery stalks, chopped • 1 tsp. red chili pepper, crushed • 4 tbs. oil for frying • 1½ cups water • Juice of ½ lemon • Salt

---

In a shallow pan heat oil. Add garlic and meat, celery, salt, water, chili pepper, and simmer over low heat for an hour. Add pitted olives, and continue to cook for another ½ hour. Five minutes before removing from heat add lemon juice. Bring to a boil once and remove.

Serve as main course, with red wine or brandy.

95   KUDOOREY BASAR B'ROTEF AGVANIYOT

MEATBALLS IN TOMATO SAUCE

NEW

Preparing time: 15 minutes. Cooking time: 30 minutes. Serves 6

---

2 lbs. minced beef • 1 small tin tomato purée • 1 tsp.
sugar • 1 onion, sliced • 3 cloves garlic • 2 eggs • Parsley
• 1 oz. flour • Salt • Pepper • Oil for frying

Sauté onion and garlic. Mince together with parsley. Place
minced meat and eggs into a bowl, add onion and garlic, and
mix well. Form meatballs of about 1 oz. each. (1 inch diameter)
Put 2 cups water into a saucepan, bring to a boil, and add
tomato purée, salt, pepper and sugar. Dilute flour in water, add
to sauce while boiling, stir and add meatballs. Cook over
medium heat for 15 mins.
Serve as a main course, with mashed potatoes and cooked
vegetables.

96   KEBAB CHAVUSHIM

GIPSY STEW

Stewed meat and quinces

TRADITIONAL for Rumanian Jews

Preparing time: 20 minutes. Cooking time: 50 minutes. Serves 6

1½ lbs. stewing beef, cubed • 5 medium quinces, cubed •
1 tbs. vinegar • 2 tbs. sugar • Oil • Salt • Pepper • 1
whole onion, peeled • 2 onions chopped

Arrange the meat in a saucepan, pour in water to cover meat,
and bring to boil on medium heat. Add onion, and continue to

cook for 15-20 mins., until meat is tender. Remove onion when it is soft. Pour out liquid from saucepan, brown meat in some oil, and add chopped onion, salt and pepper to taste. Add quinces to meat, some water, vinegar, cover pan, and continue to cook on low heat for 25 mins. until dish is ready.
Serve as main dish, with fresh salad and rice in goose or chicken fat.

97   SHISHLICK

SKEWERS OF MEAT

TRADITIONAL for Yemenite Jews

Preparing time: 20 minutes. Cooking time: 20 minutes. Serves 5

---

3 lbs. beef steak, cubed • ½ cup olive oil • 1 tsp. salt • 2 tbs. vinegar • ¼ tsp. pepper • 2 lbs. tomatoes, cubed • 2 green peppers, cut in squares • 3 large onions, sliced • Kitchen bouquet

---

Mix together olive oil, salt, vinegar and pepper. Pour over meat and vegetables, and leave in a cool place for 3 hours. On skewers arrange meat between the tomatoes, onion slices, green peppers, and brush the meat with kitchen bouquet. Turn over charcoal grill every 5 mins. until meat is tender and evenly browned.
Serve as main dish, with wine or Pernod.

98   TA'AROVET BASAR IM KRUVEET

CUBED STEW AND FLOWERETS

Meat stew with cauliflower

NEW

Preparing time: 30 minutes. Cooking time: 2½ hours. Serves 5

1½ lbs. stewing beef, cubed • 1 cauliflower (about ¼ lb.) • 2 tbs. tomato purée • ½ cup oil • 1 lemon, sliced • 1 cup water • 4 tbs. flour • 1 onion, chopped • Salt • Pepper • Oil for frying

---

Place a little oil in a saucepan, and sauté onion. Coat meat cubes in flour, add to onion, and fry until brown. Add tomato purée, and while stirring pour over water. Cook for 1½-2 hours. Clean cauliflower well, divide into flowerets, place in a saucepan, cover with water, add lemon slices, salt and pepper, and boil for 5 mins. Cool, drain, and add to meat stew. Continue to cook for 20 minutes.
Serve as main course, with boiled potatoes and peas, and vin rosé.

99   KURICH BASAR

MOUSAKA SANDWICH

Meat and vegetable sandwich

TRADITIONAL for Persian Jews

Preparing time: 30 minutes Cooking time: 30 minutes. Serves 6

1 lb. minced beef • 4 large potatoes • 2 medium onions, chopped • 5 ozs. spinach • 3 ozs. spring onion • 5 eggs • 1 medium tomato, grated • ½ cup margarine • Parsley, chopped • ½ tsp. curry powder • Pinch of cinammon • Pinch of pepper • Salt

Rinse the spinach thoroughly under running water. When clean, pour over boiling water, let cool and drain.
Peel the potatoes, and cut into thick slices. Boil for 5 mins. in salted water. Drain off liquid and let cool.
Mix minced meat with spices, spinach, onion, parsley, grated tomato and two eggs. Mix well.
Grease Pyrex dish well. In it arrange a layer of potatoes. Cover with a layer of meat. Top with remainder of potatoes. Prepare a thin mixture of three eggs, salt and pepper. Pour over the potatoes. Bake in a moderate oven until browned (with tine of fork check when potatoes are tender).
Serve hot as main course, with red wine.

100   KAVED EGEL B'NUSACH YEHUDEI HABALKAN

BALKAN MANNA

Calves' liver in vinegar sauce

TRADITIONAL for Balkanian Jews

Preparing time: 15 minutes. Cooking time: 20 minutes. Serves 6

1¼ lbs. calves' liver • ⅓ cup margarine • 3 tbs. vinegar • Parsley, chopped • Salt • Pepper

Dissolve margarine in a frying pan, place strips of liver in pan, and fry over medium heat. Add salt, pepper, parsley, vinegar diluted with some water, and stir. After vinegar evaporates, continue to fry for another 10 minutes.
Serve as a main dish, with rice in goose fat and glazed carrots.

101   MO'ACH KEVES B'NUSACH YEHUDEI HAMAGREB

PRIDE OF MAGREB

Sheep's brains, with mushroom and anchovy spread

TRADITIONAL for North African Jews

Preparing time: 30 minutes. Cooking time: 25 minutes. Serves 6

---

6 whole sheep's brains (calves brains may be substituted)
• 1 tin anchovy fillets • 1½ cups fresh mushrooms •
Parsley, chopped • ½ medium onion • 2 tbs. margarine •
1 tbs. vinegar • 1-2 chicken bouillon cubes • Salt • Pepper

Place the brains in a deep dish, and rinse under a running tap
for 10 mins. Remove to a large saucepan of water, together with
vinegar, some salt, and onion. Bring to a boil over medium
heat, remove and let cool under running tap.
Rinse mushrooms well, slice thinly, sauté in margarine, and add
a pinch of salt, pepper and the bouillon cubes. When done, place
on a wooden board, and chop together with the parsley.
Arrange brains in a baking dish. Mash anchovies, mix with a
little margarine, and spread mixture on the brains. Repeat with
mushroom spread. About ¼ hour before serving, place in hot
oven.
Serve hot, as main dish, with stewed or baked potatoes and
stewed vegetables.

102   OFF KURI YEHUDI

MOCK CURRY

Spiced meat

TRADITIONAL for Jews of India

Preparing time: 20 minutes. Cooking time: 1½ hours. Serves 6

½ lb. beef, cubed (chicken may be substituted) • 3 cups potatoes, cubed • ½ lb. onions, sliced • 3 ozs. tomato purée • ½ tsp. curry • ¼ tsp. saffron • 3 tsp. sugar • 2 tbs. lemon juice • 1 tbs. garlic powder • ⅕ cup oil for frying • Salt

Heat oil in a pan, and fry onions in it. Add tomato purée and all other ingredients, except sugar, lemon juice and potatoes. Cook for a few minutes, while stirring. Add meat, cover with water and cook over low heat until meat is tender.
Add potatoes, sugar and lemon juice. Continue to cook until potatoes are done. If liquid evaporates, add warm water for sufficient gravy. (If chicken is used in recipe, cook together with the potatoes).
Serve hot as a main dish, with cool drinks.

103   KREYSHA TRIPOLITANIA

SWEETBREADS IN LEMON SAUCE

TRADITIONAL for Tripolitanian Jews

Preparing time: 60 minutes. Cooking time: 2 ½ hours. Serves 10

Sweetbreads • 1 large head of garlic • ½ cup oil for frying • Juice of 1 lemon • 1 tsp. red hot pepper • Salt • 1 lb. new potatoes, peeled • 1 cup hot water

Clean sweetbreads thoroughly by scraping with a knife and then rinsing well. Repeat several times, until sweetbreads are clean and white. Rub on lemon juice and salt, and cut into small cubes. Fry garlic in oil, add red pepper and sweetbreads and pour over hot water. Bring to a boil, reduce heat, and simmer over very low heat, covered, for 2½ hours, or until meat is tender. During cooking you may add water gradually, if necessary. Half an hour before dish is ready, add whole

potatoes.
The Jews of Tripoli eat this dish as a main course, with brandy or arak.

104   MO'ACH B'PILPEL ADOM

SPICY BEEF'S BRAINS

TRADITIONAL for Oriental Jews

Preparing time: 10 minutes. Cooking time: 35 minutes. Serves 5

---

1 small brain • 5 cloves garlic, whole • ½ tsp. chili powder • 3 tbs. oil for frying • Parsley, chopped • Salt • 1 cup water

---

Soak brain in water until all the blood is removed. Remove skin and fibres.
Sauté garlic in oil, add chili powder, water and parsley, and bring to a boil. Add brain reduce heat, add salt to taste and cook for ½ hour, until most of the liquid has evaporated.
Serve as main course, with cooked olives and dry red wine.

105   K'TSITSAT BASAR MUKREMET

MEAT BALLS IN EGG SAUCE

NEW

Preparing time: 15 minutes. Cooking time: 20 minutes. Serves 6

> 1½ lb. minced beef • 1 onion, chopped • 1 level cup flour
> • 2 cloves garlic, minced • 5 eggs • 4 tbs. margarine •
> 2 cups water • Salt • Pepper • Oil for frying

Sauté onion and garlic. In a bowl combine meat, garlic, fried onion, 1 egg, and mix well. Form into balls, and fry in pan with little oil (just covering bottom of pan). Remove, and place in a baking dish. Prepare white sauce by melting margarine in a saucepan, add flour, stirring constantly while adding water, salt, pepper. Cook over medium heat for 10 minutes, stirring occasionally. Remove from heat. Separate 4 remaining eggs. Add yolks to white sauce, stirring constantly. Pour over meatballs. Bake in a very hot oven or under grill for a few minutes, until light brown.
Serve as main course, with mashed potatoes, carrots, peas and with vin rosé.

106 GOULASCH BASAR B'ROTEV CHATSILIM

PERSIAN GOULASH

Meat stew with eggplants

TRADITIONAL for Persian Jews

Preparing time: 20 minutes. Cooking time: 60-90 mins. Serves 6

> 1 lb. beef • 1 large eggplant • ½ cup oil for frying • 1
> onion, sliced • 3 medium tomatoes • ½ cup water • 3
> ozs. tomato purée • Juice of ½ lemon • Pinch of nutmeg
> • ¼ tsp. cinnamon • ¼ tsp. pepper

Slice unpeeled eggplant, sprinkle with salt, and let stand. Cut meat into cubes. In a shallow pan warm ⅓ of the oil. Place in sliced onion, meat and spices. Cover with lid, and let simmer

for threequarters of an hour over low heat. Cube the tomatoes, add to meat, add the ½ cup water, and let simmer for another 20 minutes.
Meanwhile drain the eggplant slices, and wipe off excess salt. Fry slices in hot oil, add to the meat, together with tomato purée. Shortly before dish is ready, add lemon juice.
Serve as main course, with rice, potatoes or macaroni.

107   TUVSHIL GOULASCH HUNGARI

HUNGARIAN GOULASH

Stewed steak and vegetables

TRADITIONAL for Hungarian Jews

Preparing time: 25 minutes. Cooking time: 2 hours. Serves 6

> 2 lbs. lean steak, cut into cubes • 3 carrots, diced • 1 onion, diced • ½ cup celery, diced • ½ cup ketchup • 2 tbs. brown sugar • 3 tbs. Worcestershire sauce • 1 tsp. paprika • 2 tbs. vinegar • ½ tsp. powdered mustard • 1 tsp. salt • 2 tbs. flour • 1 clove garlic, grated • 2 tbs. fat • 3 cups hot water • Parsley

Brown meat, onion and garlic, in fat. Set aside. Put ketchup and next six ingredients (above), in a mixing bowl. Place pan with meat and onions on a low heat. Add celery and carrots. Pour the hot water over the meat, add the rest of the ingredients from the mixing bowl, and mix well. Cover, and simmer for 2 hours. Mix the flour with cold water, and thicken gravy in pot. Garnish with parsley.
Serve as main dish, with red wine.

108 BASAR KAR

COLD CUTS

Cooked cold meat

TRADITIONAL

Preparing time: 15 minutes. Cooking time: 1½ hours. Serves 10

---

2 lbs. beef (top round, or desired cut) • ½ head of garlic
• ½ tsp. black pepper • ½ tsp. red hot pepper • 3 tbs. oil
• Salt • ½ cup water

Rinse meat, place on a flat plate or wooden board. Crush garlic, adding spices and oil. WIth a sharp knife make cuts in the meat, insert spice mixture in cuts, using a teaspoon. Also rub some of mixture over meat.
Place meat in pressure cooker with ½ cup water. Cook over very low heat for 1½ hours. Remove from heat. Place in a flat Pyrex dish, and set aside. When it has lost its heat, transfer to refrigerator to cool.
Slice and serve with mustard and pickled cucumbers.
Serve as a main dish with warmed gravy and side dishes.

109 TASS BASAR KAR

T. V. DINNER

Cold meat plate and vegetable sauce

NEW

Preparing time: 25 minutes. Cooking time: 3 hours. Serves 8

> 2 lbs. lean beef • 4 cloves garlic • 1 large tomato, cut •
> 1 large onion • 1 green pepper • ½ cup ketchup • 1 cup
> white wine • 3 bay leaves • ½ tsp. rosemary, crushed •
> 3 cups water • 2 tsp. flour • Paprika • Salt

Place meat in saucepan of water, add tomato, green pepper, onion, bay leaves, garlic, rosemary, salt and paprika, and cook for two hours. Add wine and ketchup, and continue to cook for another hour. Remove meat, and set aside to cool. Cut into slices, and pour over the vegetable sauce.
Serve on an oval platter, with crackers, pickles and cold beer.

VEGETABLE SAUCE

Force vegetables and gravy, left over in saucepan, through a sieve. Prepare a batter from the flour and water, bring to a boil together with strained vegetables, stirring steadily until mixture thickens. Keep sauce in refrigerator, to be used with rice, potatoes, macaroni, etc.

110   MA'EUDA MAROKA'IT

MOROCCAN HAMBURGER

TRADITIONAL for Moroccan Jews

Preparing time: 25-30 mins. Cooking time: 10 minutes. Serves 5

> ½ lb. beef • 3 eggs • ¼ tsp. cayenne pepper • ¼ tsp.
> black pepper • ¼ cup oil for frying • Salt

Cook meat in water until tender. Remove meat. Chop and fry in 2 tbs. oil. Cool and add eggs and seasoning. Place the meat in a greased Pyrex dish. Pour over remainder of oil and oil from pan and bake in oven for 20-30 minutes, until it turns a golden color. (This dish is prepared on charcoal by Moroccans). Serve for light meals, with no side dishes.

111 CHALAT BASAR YEHI'AM

MEAT LOAF

Spicy meat loaf with eggs

NEW

Preparing time: 30 minutes. Cooking time: 30 minutes. Serves 8

---

2 lbs. beef for mincing • 1 large onion, sliced • ½ cup
parsley, chopped • 1 large celery leaf, chopped • 2-3 eggs
• 1 small potato, peeled • 1 slice bread • 2 tbs. tomato
purée • Pinch of black pepper • ½ tsp. cinnamon • ¼ tsp.
oregano • ¼ cup water • Pinch of hot paprika • 3 cloves
garlic • 2-3 lettuce leaves • 1 egg, hard-boiled • Oil for
frying • Salt

Sauté onion in oil until golden. Grind meat together with fried
onion, potato, hard-boiled egg, parsley, celery, garlic and slice
of bread, previously soaked in water and drained.
Mix well, add the spices, eggs, and continue to mix until
smooth. Divide mixture into two, and form two large loaves.
Grease a loaf pan and place meat loaves inside. Bake in a hot
oven for a few minutes, then reduce heat and continue to bake
for 25 minutes. Combine 1 tbs. tomato purée, water and hot
paprika, mix well and spread thinly over meat loaves. Repeat
spreading 2-3 times during baking. When meat is almost ready,
pour over remainder of tomato purée, and bake for five more
minutes. Arrange slices of loaf on flat plates, pour over some
of the gravy and decorate with lettuce leaves.
Serve as main course with baked potatoes or boiled rice, with
red wine or rosé.

112   SNIAH

MEAT CHUNKS

Baked meat and vegetables

TRADITIONAL

Preparing time: 15 minutes. Cooking time: 60 mins. Serves 5-6

> 1 lb. beef, cubed • 4 ripe tomatoes, sliced • 2 summer squash, cubed • 1 small eggplant, cubed • 3 potatoes peeled and cubed • 1 small onion, chopped • Salt • Pepper • 3 tbs. oil

Grease a baking dish, and place in all onion. Top with a layer of vegetables (but not the tomatoes), add layer of meat, and repeat layers in this order until used up. Top with slices of tomatoes, pour over oil, and sprinkle with salt and pepper. Bake in a moderate oven for an hour, until meat is tender. Serve hot, as main course.

Sweets & Desserts

113 MA'ADAN ZICHRON YAAKOV

CREAM OF CARMEL

Whipped cream delicacy, with wine mixture

NEW

Preparing time: 20 minutes. Cooking time: 5-10 mins. Serves 6

---

3 egg yolks • 2 egg whites • 6 tbs. sweet red wine • 3 tbs. sugar • 8 ozs. whipped cream • 6 lady fingers

---

Place egg yolks, wine and sugar in a saucepan, over very low heat. Whip with eggbeater, until mixture thickens. Remove from heat, and continue to whip until cold. Beat 2 egg whites. Fold into mixture, together with whipped cream, stirring slowly with a wooden spoon.
Pour into champagne glasses. Place in refrigerator.
Serve cold, decorated with a lady finger per portion, as dessert or snack.

114 SHARON HAALIZA

GAY SHARON

Chocolate soufflé

NEW

Preparing time: 15 minutes. Cooking time: 40 minutes. Serves 6

1¼ cups milk • ⅓ cup sugar • ¼ cup flour • ¾ cup cocoa • 2 tbs. butter • 3 egg yolks • 4 egg whites

---

Boil the milk with sugar, and then turn to very low heat. Mix flour with 1-2 tsps. cold milk, into a batter. Add batter gradually into warm milk, stirring slowly until texture is even and smooth. Remove from heat, add cocoa, butter, and continue to stir. Let cool. Add yolks, stirring well. Beat the egg whites until stiff. Fold into mixture.
Grease a soufflé or baking dish with butter, sprinkle some sugar over, pour in the mixture, and bake in moderate oven for 30 minutes.
Serve hot, as dessert, with glasses of cold water.

115 RAFREFET SHOKOLAD B'NUSACH CHADASH

CHOCOLATE DREAM

Chocolate custard with almonds

NEW

Preparing time: 35-40 minutes. Cooking time: 1 hour. Serves 6

2½ ozs. chocolate, grated • 4 ozs. plain cookies • 1 tbs. almonds, shelled • 1 pint milk • ⅓ cup sugar • 5 egg yolks • 3 egg whites • 1 tbs. butter

---

Pour milk into saucepan, and place over medium heat. Add sugar and grated chocolate, and melt while stirring constantly. When chocolate is dissolved, remove from heat.

Blanch almonds by placing them in boiling water, and remove skins by hand. Dry well, and crush together with cookies. Add to milk, and set aside to cool. Add yolks to milk, stirring well. Beat egg whites, and fold into milk mixture.

Grease small pan with butter, sprinkle with some sugar, pour in the mixture and cover.

Place pan in larger pan half filled with hot water, and put the pan in a moderate oven for an hour. Take out of oven, and let cool for 10 minutes. After cooling, remove chocolate from pan and divide into serving bowls.

Serve warm or cold, as dessert.

116   TAPUCHAI EDEN

APPLES OF EDEN

Stuffed apples, with dried fruit

NEW

Preparing time: 20 minutes. Cooking time: 30 minutes. Serves 6

6 large apples • ¾ cup sultanas • ½ cup white wine • Rind of 1 orange • ¼ cup butter • ½ cup granulated sugar

Wash the apples thoroughly, and remove cores. Grease a baking dish with butter, and arrange apples in it.

Rinse sultanas well, boil for a few seconds in ¼ cup wine. Stuff apples with sultanas, top with dried peel, a few chips of butter and a sprinkling of sugar.

Pour wine carefully over each apple, and bake in a moderate oven for ½ hour.

Serve hot, with cold water to drink.

117   OREZ MIZRACHI

ORIENTAL RICE PUDDING

TRADITIONAL

Preparing time: 10 minutes. Cooking time: 35 minutes. Serves 6

¼ cup rice • 1 cup water • 3 cups milk • 2½ tbs. sugar
• Rosewater • Pinch of salt • Cinnamon

In a saucepan combine water, milk, sugar and salt. When boiling
point is reached, add rice, and let cook on low heat for 25
minutes. Add a few drops rosewater, and continue to cook for
another five minutes, or until all liquid is absorbed and rice
is ready.
Place in bowls and put in refrigerator to chill.
Before serving top with cinnamon and sugar.
Serve as dessert, or for breakfast.

118   MA'ADAN EMEK HAYARDEN

JORDAN VALLEY DELICACY

Fried bananas in citrus sauce

NEW

Preparing time: 15 minutes. Cooking time: 15 minutes. Serves 6

---

6 firm bananas • Peel of 1 orange, grated • Peel of 1
lemon, grated • 1 tbs. lemon juice • 2 tbs. orange juice •
⅓ cup butter • 3 tbs. brandy • 2 tbs. sugar

Peel bananas, and halve them, lengthwise. Melt butter in a hot
frying pan, add sugar and grated peel. Continue to fry for a

short time. Add bananas, and fry on both sides.
Pour brandy over, and set it alight. When the flames die down, add orange and lemon juice, and continue to fry until juice evaporates.
Remove from heat, and serve while hot, as dessert.

119   CHAVITAT EGOZEI KOKOS

PANCAKES STUFFED WITH COCONUTS & RAISINS

TRADITIONAL for Jews of India

Preparing time: 10 minutes. Cooking time: 15 minutes. Serves 6

---

3 cups flour • 1½ cups sugar • 1½ cups milk • 3 ozs. raisins • ½ lb. shredded coconut • 3 eggs • 1 oz. vanilla sugar • Oil

---

In a bowl combine flour, sugar, vanilla sugar and milk. Mix well.
Beat eggs and add to mixture.
Grease a frying pan lightly, place on low heat, and when hot pour in 1 tbs. of batter. Tilt pan to allow batter to cover pan entirely. Remove, and repeat until all batter is used.
Place some coconut mixed with raisins on the fried side of pancake. Roll around raisins, and return to pan to brown lightly.
Serve hot as a dessert, or for late meals.
See photograph on page 97.

120   RAFREFET PRI GINA

STRAWBERRY ICES

NEW

Preparing time: 1½ hours. Serves 6

1½ lbs. whole strawberries • Juice of 2 lemons • Juice of 1 orange • 1½ pints water • 2 cups sugar

---

Rinse strawberries well. Boil water with sugar, and pour in a bowl to cool. In an electric blender mix strawberries, lemon and orange juice, and add to water in bowl. Pour mixture into icetrays, place trays in refrigerator, but not in freezer, and chill for at least 2 hours. The mixture should not be allowed to freeze.
Serve as dessert or refreshment.

121   CHAVITANIONET

FRUITJACKS

Pancakes stuffed with fresh fruit

NEW

Preparing time: 10 minutes. Frying and baking time: 20 minutes. Serves 6

---

7 ozs. flour • 4 eggs • 6 egg whites • Fresh fruit • 1 cup milk • ½ cup sugar • 1 tbs. oil for frying • 1 jigger of liqueur • 6 cherries

---

Beat 4 eggs, and add flour gradually, beating well. Add milk, 1 tsp. sugar, oil, and whip batter well. Pass through a strainer, to avoid lumps. Prepare pancakes, and set aside to cool.
Cut fruit into small cubes, and mix in liqueur. Place some of

the fruit mixture on each pancake, and roll. Arrange pancakes in a baking dish.

Beat 6 egg whites with remainder of sugar. Pour mixture over pancakes, and bake in a very hot oven, until egg whites set, and turn a dark gold color.

Decorate dish with cherries, and serve hot, as dessert.

122   RAFREFET HADAGAN

CREAMED ORANGE

Cream of Wheat in orange juice

NEW

Preparing time: 10 minutes. Cooking time: 5 minutes. Serves 5

> 3 tbs. Cream of Wheat • 1 cup water • 1 cup natural orange juice • 3 tbs. sugar • ½ tsp. rum • Raspberry syrup (or 5 cherries)

In a saucepan combine Cream of Wheat, sugar and water. Bring to a boil, and continue to cook over very low heat, stirring constantly until Cream of Wheat thickens. Add orange juice gradually, while stirring. When boiling point is reached, remove from heat.

Pour mixture into an electric blender, add rum and blend until mixture becomes creamy.

Serve as dessert, topping mixture with raspberry syrup or a cherry.

123   MA'ADAN CHAG

HOLIDAY ORIENTAL

Nut dessert

TRADITIONAL for Jews from India

Preparing time: 10 minutes. Cooking time: 10 minutes. Serves 8

> 1 oz. gelatine • 1 cup sugar • 2 cups milk • 2 cups water • 1 tsp. cinnamon • 1 cup nuts, chopped (walnuts or pistachios)

Put milk, water and sugar into a pan. Add gelatine, stirring constantly. When gelatine dissolves, remove from heat, pour into dessert dishes, sprinkle with cinnamon and nuts.
Serve cold as dessert or snack.

124   RAFREFET B'GLIDA

VANILLA ICE N'RUM

NEW

Preparing time: 15 minutes. Serves 6

> 2 pints vanilla ice cream • ⅕ cup walnuts, crushed • ⅕ cup almonds, crushed • ⅓ cup sultanas • ¼ cup rum • 4 egg whites • 2 egg yolks • 3 tbs. sugar • 3 squares chocolate, grated • Lady fingers

Place grated chocolate in a Pyrex bowl, pour ¼ cup boiling water over, and let dissolve. Mix in the rum. Beat egg whites with sugar, until stiff. Fold in the melted chocolate and the egg yolks. Place helpings of ice cream on small, flat plates, cover with chocolate mixture, and top with raisins and nuts.

Decorate with lady fingers.
Serve as dessert, with cold drinks.

125 GAVIA HAFTA'AT GLIDA

FRUIT AND WINE CASSATA

NEW

Preparing time: 15 minutes. Serves 6

> 2 slices lemon • 2 tbs. cherry liqueur • 12 cherries, pitted
> • 1 oz. sultanas • 2½ pints vanilla ice-cream • 1 cup
> whipped cream • 1 tsp. vanilla extract • Confectioner's
> sugar • 1½ slices pineapple • 6 cherries • Pinch of
> cinnamon

Blend the fruit, liqueur, vanilla extract and lemon slices in
electric blender, until foamy. In a bowl mix the blended fruit
with ice cream. Arrange in ice-trays, and place in refrigerator
to freeze. Before serving, cut into portions. Top with whipped
cream, and sprinkle with confectioner's sugar and cinnamon.
To serve, decorate with a cherry or a quarter-slice pineapple.
Serve as a dessert or snack, with cool drinks.

126 GALIL CHAVITAH MEMULAH PRI

EGG N'APPLE

Rolled omelette stuffed with baked apples

NEW

Preparing time: 15 minutes. Cooking time: 40 minutes. Serves 6

> 5 medium apples • 6 eggs • 3 tbs. milk • Oil for frying
> • 2 tbs. sugar

Beat eggs well, while adding milk. Peel the apples, and core. Arrange apples in a baking dish, sprinkle with sugar, and bake for 30 minutes.
Fry beaten eggs in a greased frying pan, on very low heat, for 7-10 minutes on one side only. Let cool.
Mash the baked apples, arrange in the omelette, roll and put in refrigerator until serving.
Cut into portions, and serve cold as dessert.

127 DIESA SURIT

DAMASCUS PORRIDGE

Sweet porridge, with rosewater

TRADITIONAL for Syrian Jews

Preparing time: 10 minutes. Cooking time: 5 minutes. Serve 5

> ⅔ cup Cream of Wheat • 4 tbs. margarine • ½ cup sugar
> • 1 cup water • Cinnamon • Rosewater • 2-3 lbs. chopped
> nuts

Brown the Cream of Wheat in hot margarine. Add sugar and pour in water gradually. Cook for 10 minutes, until cereal has smooth texture. Remove from heat, pour into shallow bowls, and set aside to cool. Sprinkle each serving with rosewater and cinnamon. If desired, decorate with chopped nuts.
Serve cold as a dessert.

KERMAN/KERMAN

Cakes, Cookies & Pastry

128 DUVSHANIT

HONEY CAKE AND NUTS

NEW

Preparing time: 30 minutes. Baking time: 35 minutes.

> 1 cup self-rising flour • 1 cup sugar • 5 eggs • Pinch of salt • ½ tsp. cinnamon • ½ tsp. ground cloves • ½ lb. walnuts, chopped • ¼ tsp. baking soda • Syrup (see below)

Beat the egg whites until stiff. In another bowl combine 1 cup sugar, egg yolks, salt, flour and most of the nuts. Mix well, to a smooth dough. Add cloves, baking soda and cinnamon, and continue to mix. Fold in egg whites lightly. Place on a greased baking sheet, and bake in a moderate oven for 35 minutes. Remove and pour over syrup while cake is still warm.
Decorate with remaining chopped nuts.

SYRUP

> 1 cup sugar • 3 cups water • 1 cup honey

Combine water and 1 cup sugar in a saucepan, and boil for 10 minutes. Add honey, stirring thoroughly. Remove from heat and let cool. This cake will keep for as long as two weeks. The longer it stands, the tastier it is.

129   UGAT PEREG

POPPY PASTRIES

Puffed pastry filled with poppy seeds and jam

NEW

Preparing time: 15 minutes. Baking time: 25 minutes.

> 3 cups flour • 1 tbs. sugar • ¾ cup margarine • 2 eggs • 3½ tsps. cake form yeast • Pinch of salt • ¼ cup lukewarm water

Dissolve yeast in lukewarm water, add pinch of salt and 1 tbs. sugar, and set aside. In a bowl place flour, form a hollow in the center, and place in eggs, margarine and dissolved yeast. Knead into a smooth mixture with elastic consistency, and place in refrigerator for 30 minutes.

FILLING

> ¾ cup poppy seeds • ¾ cup sugar • 2 tbs. jam. • Vanilla sugar • ⅓ cup water

Place poppy seeds in a saucepan, add sugar, water, and cook until mixture is almost thick. Remove and let cool. Add jam and vanilla sugar.
Remove pastry from refrigerator, flatten into a large leaf, spread filling on, and roll. Bake in a moderate oven for 20 minutes.

130 BAKLAWAH

COOKIES WITH NUTS AND SYRUP

TRADITIONAL for Iraqi Jews

Preparing time: 15 minutes. Cooking time: 20 minutes.

> 1 packet puff-pastry • 2½ cups peanuts (or almonds or walnuts), chopped • 1 cup unsalted margarine • 2 cups sugar • ½ cup water

Divide pastry into quarters. In a baking dish put a layer of pastry, sprinkle some chopped nuts over, top with layer of pastry, and repeat until pastry is all used. Use a knife to cut into diamond shapes. Grate hard margarine over pastry, and bake in a moderate oven until cookies are light brown. Remove, and let cool for 15 minutes.
Boil water, add sugar and mix until thick syrup is formed. Pour hot syrup immediately over cookies, using a spoon.
Serve as a dessert or snack, with semi-sweet Turkish coffee.
See photograph on page 128.

131   MA'AMOOL

THE SULTAN'S TURRETS

Stuffed cookies with nuts

TRADITIONAL for Oriental Jews

Preparing time: 45 minutes. Baking time: 15-20 minutes.

---

3 cups flour • 1 cup walnuts, chopped • 1 tbs. cinnamon • 1 cup oil, or 7 ozs. margarine • 1 cup lukewarm water • ½ cup sugar • Confectioner's sugar • ¼ tsp. salt

---

In a bowl combine flour, oil or margarine, water and salt. Knead well until a smooth, soft pastry is reached.
Mix nuts with sugar and cinnamon. Roll egg-size pieces of pastry into triangles. Place 1 tbs. nuts in the center of each piece. Pinch sides together, into a pyramid shape. Arrange on a greased baking sheet, leaving space between cookies. Bake in medium-high oven for few minutes, then reduce to medium heat, until cookies turn a golden color. Baking should not take more than 15-20 minutes.
Remove from oven, sprinkle each cookie with confectioner's sugar, and place on a flat tray to cool.
Serve with hot drinks (semi-sweet Turkish coffee recommended).
See photograph on page 125.

132   MA'AROUD

COOKIES TAMAR

Cookies stuffed with dates

TRADITIONAL for Oriental Jews

Preparing time: 30 minutes. Baking time: 15-18 minutes.

Pastry (see recipe 131, THE SULTAN'S TURRETS) • 1 lb. dates, pitted • 1 level tbs. cinnamon • 1 tsp. cloves, ground • ¼ tsp. nutmeg • Confectioner's sugar

Warm dates in a pan, until soft. Add spices, and blend well until even texture is reached. Form into balls.
Take apple-size pieces of dough, and roll. Spread the date mixture thickly (about one-fifth inch) on the dough, and roll up. With a sharp knife, make thin, small cuts along the roll. Cut into 1 inch thick slices, diagonally, and arrange on a greased baking sheet, so cookies do not touch. Bake in a moderate-high oven for a few minutes; reduce to medium heat, and bake until a light brown color. Baking should not take more than 18 minutes. Remove, sprinkle confectioner's sugar on each cookie, and place on flat plate to cool.
Serve with hot drinks (semi-sweet Turkish coffee, with cold water, is recommended).

133   LEVIVOT TEH RUSIOT

RUSSIAN DOUGHNUTS

TRADITIONAL for Russian Jews

Preparing time: 1½ hours. Frying time: 10-15 minutes.

1 lb. flour • 2 eggs • 1 cup sour milk (at room temperature) • 1 tbs. sugar • ½ oz. cake form yeast • ¼ cup lukewarm water • Salt • Oil for frying • Confectioner's sugar

Mix yeast and sugar in water, and let stand in a warm place. In a bowl combine flour, eggs, sour milk, dissolved yeast mixture, and pinch of salt. Stir well with a wooden spoon to a smooth dough. Cover with a towel and put in a warm place

for 2 hours, for dough to rise.
Drop doughnuts in deep, hot oil, using a spoon. Fry until golden.
Remove and place on absorbent paper to drain. Sprinkle with
confectioner's sugar, and serve hot.
Russion Jews eat these doughnuts, while drinking large quanti-
ties of tea from a samovar placed on the table.

134   T'FICHAT DVASH

HONEY DUMPLINGS

TRADITIONAL for Greek Jews

Preparing time: 25 minutes. Frying time: 5-7 minutes.

> 2 cups self-rising flour • 8 eggs • 2 cups water • 3 ozs.
> margarine • Peel of 1 lemon • ½ cup honey • Oil for
> deep frying • Salt • Cinnamon

Combine 2 cups water, margarine and lemon peel, and bring
to a boil for 2 mins. Remove from heat and immediately take
out lemon peel. Add the flour and pinch of salt together, stirring vigorously to prevent lumps.
Return to fire, and cook over low heat for 5 mins., stirring
constantly until a non-sticky dough is formed. Remove from
heat and let cool. Add eggs, one by one, stirring all the while
until mixture is smooth. In a deep pan heat oil. Using a table-
spoon drop in the batter, a spoonful at a time, and fry until
golden. Remove and place on a towel to drain off excess oil.
Combine honey and a little water, pour this over the dumplings,
and sprinkle them with plenty of cinnamon.
Serve as a dessert, or snack with strong, hot tea.

135   UGIYOT S'DOM

PIQUANT PASTRY

Puff Pastry with cheese

NEW

Preparing time: 15 minutes. Baking time: 20 minutes.

> ½ lb. self-rising flour • 1 cup margarine • 1 cup yellow
> cheese, (Cheddar or Parmesan), grated • 3 egg yolks •
> ½ cup sour cream • ¼ tsp. salt • ¼ tsp. caraway seeds,
> ground • Pinch of pepper.

In a bowl combine flour, sour cream grated cheese, 2 egg yolks
and seasoning. Knead into a dough, and place in the refrigerator
for 2-3 hours. Sprinkle flour over a board, and roll dough into
a sheet about ½-inch thick. Using a glass tumbler, press out
circles. Place on a greased baking sheet, brush with egg yolk,
and bake in a moderate oven for 20 mins.

136   SUMBOOSAK

Pastry stuffed with spinach and cheese

TRADITIONAL for Lebanese Jews

Preparing time: 45 minutes. Cooking time: 30 minutes.

> 2 lbs. flour • 1 egg • 1 cup margarine, or ½ cup oil • 1
> cup lukewarm water • 6 tbs. yeast • 1 tsp. sugar • Salt

A. PASTRY

Place yeast and sugar in a cup of lukewarm water for 5 mins.
Put flour in a large bowl, and in the center add yeast, egg and

water, margarine and a pinch of salt. Knead well, until a smooth dough (not sticky) is formed. Add more lukewarm water if necessary. From dough form a ball. Sprinkle with salt, cover with a towel, and let stand. Roll pieces of dough (egg-size) thinly.

B. SPINACH STUFFING

---

1 lb. spinach • ¾ cup Cheddar or Parmesan, grated •
1 large onion, finely chopped • ¼ tsp. black pepper

Wash spinach thoroughly, place in a bowl with hot water to cover until it softens. Shred thinly, and mix well with cheese, onion, and black pepper, using a wooden spoon.
Place spoonful of spinach in center of each piece of dough, fold in two, and pinch edges closed. Let stand for 20 minutes to rise. Arrange pieces of dough in a greased sheet, so they do not touch. Bake in a medium-high oven, for a few minutes. Reduce to medium heat. Baking should not take longer than 20-30 minutes. Pieces are ready when they turn a brownish colour.
Serve together with stewed meat, or as first course, with brandy or Pernod.

137   BOREKAHS

PUFFED PASTRY, STUFFED WITH CHEESE

TRADITIONAL   for Syrian Jews

Preparing time: 1½ hours. Cooking time: 30 minutes.

---

1 lb. flour • 4 tbs. oil • Juice of 1 lemon • 1¾ cups water •
1 cup margarine • 1 tsp. salt

In a deep bowl combine flour, oil, lemon juice, water and salt. Knead into a dough. Sprinkle some flour on a board, and roll the dough. Spread margarine over, fold dough into envelope shape, and place in refrigerator for ½ hour.
Remove from refrigerator and repeat rolling. Close dough into envelope shape, replace in refrigerator for ½ hour. Repeat this procedure once more. Remove from refrigerator a third time, after ½ hour, and roll dough into a large, thin leaf.

STUFFING

2 potatoes, boiled in jackets • ½ lb. hard yellow cheese (Cheddar or Parmesan), grated • 2 eggs • 1 tbs. margarine • 5 ozs. sesame seeds

Peel potatoes, and mash. Add grated cheese, one egg, 1 tbs. margarine, and mix well.
Cut 1 thinly rolled dough into 3-inch squares. Place a teaspoon of stuffing in each square, and pinch closed into a triangular shape. Brush each pastry with beaten egg, and sprinkle with sesame seeds. Bake in a moderate oven for 30 mins, or until golden.
Serve as first course, or snack with coffee. (Syrian Jews eat the borekahs with fresh vegetable salad, on Friday afternoons, as a pre-Sabbath meal).
See photograph on page 127.

138   KA'ACHEI SUMSUM

BAGEL COOKIES

Salted sesame cookies

TRADITIONAL for Syrian Jews

Preparing time: 40 minutes. Baking time: 20-30 minutes.

4 cups flour • 1 cup margarine • 1 tsp. salt • 3 tbs. cake form yeast • 1 egg • 3 ozs. sesame seeds • 1 cup lukewarm water • ¼ tsp. sugar

Place yeast and sugar in a bowl. Pour over lukewarm water. Put in a warm place for 10 mins., until yeast rises.
Prepare a dough from flour, margarine, salt and dissolved yeast mixture. Cover dough with a towel, put in a warm place for 2 hours. When dough rises, take small pieces and roll into strips about 4 ins. long. Join the ends to form a bagel. Brush each one with beaten egg, coat with sesame seeds, and place on a greased baking sheet. Arrange bagels in rows, leaving a space between each one. Bake in a moderate oven for 20-30 mins.
The bagels are eaten for Sabbath breakfast, with coffee, by Syrian Jews.
See photograph on page 115.

TABLES OF WEIGHTS, MEASURES AND TEMPERATURES

WEIGHT	COMMODITY	MEASURE
4 ounces	Almonds (shelled)	1 cup
4 ounces	Apple purée	3½ tablespoons
4 ounces	Bread crumbs	1 cup
1 pound	Beans	2 cups
½ pound	Butter (or margarine)	1 cup
½ ounce	Butter (or margarine)	1 tablespoon
1 pound	Corn meal	3 cups
1 pound	Corn starch	4 cups
1 ounce	Corn starch	2 tablespoons
1 ounce	Cocoa	3½ tablespoons
1 pound	Cream of Wheat	2½ cups
1 ounce	Curry powder	3½ tablespoons
1 pound	Flour	4 cups
1 ounce	Flour	2 tablespoons
½ ounce	Flour	3 teaspoons
1 pint	Milk	2 cups
8 ounces	Meat (minced)	1 cup
4 ounces	Mushrooms (chopped)	1 cup
4 ounces	Peanuts	1 cup
3 ounces	Poppy seeds	1 cup
1 pound	Potatoes (mashed)	2 cups
1 pound	Raisins	3 cups
1 pound	Rice (dry)	2½ cups
1 pound	Rice (boiled)	3 cups
3 ounces	Sesame seeds	1 cup
1 ounce	Soup powder	1 tablespoon
1 pound	Spinach (cooked and mashed)	1½ cups
1 pound	Sugar (granulated)	2 cups
1 ounce	Sugar	1 tablespoon
1 ounce	Syrup	1 tablespoon
4 ounces	Techina	3½ tablespoons
4 ounces	Tomato purée	3½ tablespoons

WEIGHT	COMMODITY	MEASURE
8 ounces	Tomato juice	1 cup
4 ounces	Walnuts (shelled)	1 cup
1 ounce	Yeast (compressed)	1 square
1 ounce	Yeast	½ cup
1 pound	=	16 ounces
1 pint	=	2 cups
1 cup	=	16 tablespoons
1 tablespoon	=	3 teaspoons

OVEN TEMPERATURES

Temperature gauge	Oven temp. (F°)	Oven temp. (C°)	Thermostat
Very low — low	200 — 300	93 — 148	¼ , ½, 1, 2
Medium low — moderate	300 — 350	148 — 176	3
Moderate	350 — 375	176 — 190	4
Medium high — high	375 — 450	190 — 232	5, 6, 7
Very high	450 — 500	232 — 315	8, 9

INDEX